THE ESSENTIAL TAO

THE ESSENTIAL

TAO

An Initiation
into the Heart of Taoism
Through the Authentic *Tao Te Ching*
and the Inner Teachings of *Chuang-tzu*

translated and presented by
THOMAS CLEARY

HarperSanFrancisco
A Division of HarperCollins*Publishers*

84 9093

FIRST EDITION

Library of Congress Cataloging-in-Publication Data
Cleary, Thomas F.
  The essential Tao : an initiation into the heart of Taoism through the authentic Tao te ching and the inner teachings of Chuang Tzu / translated and presented by Thomas Cleary. — 1st ed.
      p.   cm.
  Includes bibliographical references.
  ISBN 0-06-250162-3 (alk. paper)
  1. Taoism.   2. Lao-tzu. Tao te ching.   3. Chuang-tzu. Nan-hua ching.   I. Lao-tzu. Tao te ching. English. 1992.   II. Chuang-tzu. Nan-hua ching. English. 1992.   III. Title.
  BL1910.C63 1992
  299'.51482—dc20   91-55283
                                                                          CIP

92 93 94 95 96 MART 10 9 8 7 6 5 4 3 2 1

This edition is printed on acid-free paper that meets the American National Standards Institute Z39.48 Standard.

Contents

Introduction

Tao is one of the most basic and comprehensive symbols in the Chinese language, the center of all philosophical and spiritual discourse. It may mean a path, a way, a principle, a method, a doctrine, a system of order; and it also may mean the matrix, structure, and reality of the universe itself. Every art and science is called a tao, or a way; but the source of everything, the fountain of all art and science, is called the Tao, or the Way.

Taoism is based, first and foremost, on the experience of this universal Way, the essential reality through which all derivative ways might be comprehended.

Considering the ultimate nature of the Way to be inherently beyond the bounds of human conception, ancient Taoists sought traces of the Way in the patterns of events taking place in the natural world, the social world, and the inner world of the individual psyche. Eventually the scope of the Way led them to undertake the investigation of vast domains of knowledge and experience.

While followers of Taoism thus branched out into many different fields of research and work, those interested primarily in the essential Tao continued to focus on perfecting the mastery of human nature and life in three critical areas: individual well-being, social harmony, and accelerated evolution of consciousness. These three bases were believed to form the foundation of overall human development, the guiding lights of the arts and sciences.

Through generations of applying the Tao to these three basic domains of life, extraordinary accomplishments in the maintenance of physical vitality, fostering of sensitive and effective relations between people, and development of latent mental powers, including spontaneous insight and foreknowledge, came to be recognized as by-products of working with the Way.

Furthermore, according to the ethos of the Way, these developments, once realized, were not to be guarded possessively but put to the service of humanity. In accordance with the elusive nature of the Way, the beneficial results of its application by individuals were not to be paraded proudly before others but to be diffused in an inconspicuous yet effective manner.

There are two classic Chinese books describing the essential philosophy and practice of the Tao, made public long ago as maps of the way to the Way: *Tao Te Ching* and *Chuang-tzu*. Both these works have long outgrown cultural boundaries and are widely regarded as classics of world literature.

Composed over two thousand years ago, *Tao Te Ching* and *Chuang-tzu* are among the world's most ancient and honored books of practical wisdom. Their subject matter ranges widely, from politics and economy to psychology and mysticism, addressing the needs and interests of a diverse readership. Few of the world's great books have achieved the perennial currency of these writings.

The *Tao Te Ching* is an anthology of ancient sayings, poems, and proverbs; its compilation is attributed to the prototypical Lao-tzu, "The Old Master," who is regarded as one of the greatest ancestors of Taoism. *Chuang-tzu,* traditionally said to have been written by a Taoist named Chuang Chou, is a collection of stories and monologues illustrating and expounding the teachings of the *Tao Te Ching.* Together they present the philosophical and practical core of classical Taoism.

The *Tao Te Ching* is commonly believed to have been compiled around 500 B.C., near the end of the Spring and Autumn era, when the social and political order of China was disintegrating rapidly. The *Chuang-tzu* was written about 300 B.C., during the era of the Warring States, when the classical civilization of China was all but destroyed by civil wars.

By the middle of the second century B.C., after the unification of China, *Tao Te Ching* was firmly established at the imperial court as a favorite sourcebook of practical wisdom. The more arcane *Chuang-tzu* was transmitted in Taoist circles, as evidenced in the appearance of many allusions to it in later Taoist works of the pre-Christian era, eventually to emerge in the third century A.D. as a popular classic of deep learning ranked with *I Ching* and *Tao Te Ching*.

Ever since that time, virtually all literate people in China have read *Tao Te Ching* and *Chuang-tzu*. Countless readers have found endless fascination and enlightenment in the pregnant aphorisms and fantastic allegories of these ancient classics.

Over the centuries the *Tao Te Ching* in particular has inspired many social and spiritual movements as well as a vast body of exegetical literature. Various traditions on this text evolved among Taoist, Buddhist, Confucian, Legalist, and Martial schools of thought.

At one time, state colleges of mysticism were even established by the Chinese government for study of the philosophy of *Tao Te Ching*. People who had mastered it were sought as advisers by all kinds of people from emperors to peasants. When the Taoist canon was put to the torch by the order of the Mongol ruler of China in 1280, this *Tao Te Ching* alone was spared destruction.

Although commonly associated with Taoism, this classic was actually studied and transmitted by all of the main streams of Chinese philosophy. Commentators on it include mystics, poets, statesmen, and martial artists; numerous separate works have also been written based on some of its ideas. Over the centuries this single text spawned a vast and complex literature, reflecting the many levels of meaning revealed and concealed within its ancient sayings.

Tao Te Ching has been translated countless times into Western languages, including English, French, German, Italian,

Russian, Turkish, and Latin. It was first rendered into English more than one hundred years ago and has been retranslated, paraphrased, and adapted dozens of times since then. This volume on the essential Tao presents a new annotated English version of this classic text translated from the original Chinese.

Chuang-tzu also ranks as one of the most famous works of Chinese literature as well as being an essential Taoist sourcebook. It contains the works of different authors believed to be followers of the school of Chuang Chou, but its seven core chapters are attributed to Chuang Chou himself. He was the earliest known expositor of the teachings of Lao-tzu, and is himself numbered among the foremost masters of Taoist philosophy.

Chuang Chou was a deep thinker and a brilliant writer. He could be magnificent and grandiose, outrageous and funny, sharp and acerbic, dreamy and playful, sober and earnest, serene and unruffled. The inner meanings of his allegories have been pondered for centuries.

Throughout Chuang Chou's lifetime China was at war with itself. With several states of the ancient Chinese federation contending among themselves for territory and dominion, the whole land was caught up in an atmosphere of militarism, intrigue, and aggression. Professional strategists and martial artists roamed from state to state trying to sell their own plans for hegemony, while the people were taxed to the limit and conscripted into forced labor and military service.

Born into the midst of all this, Chuang Chou took to the ancient Way of Taoism taught in Lao-tzu's *Tao Te Ching*. Because Lao-tzu wrote extensively on the philosophy and art of enlightened leadership, as a Taoist scholar Chuang Chou was once asked to become the adviser of a king. Living in a more turbulent time than the ancient sage Lao-tzu, Chuang Chou declined the invitation, explaining that he did not care to be like a sacrificial animal fattened and dressed for slaughter.

His refusal to enter the service of a particular king notwithstanding, on examination of his writings it is clear that

Chuang Chou was not the escapist or anarchist he has often been made out to be. He was a champion of liberty, but his work is addressed to the purpose of furthering the general welfare of humanity through the edification and enlightenment of public servants as well as private individuals.

The relatively cautious and retiring attitude in dealing with worldly tyranny Chuang Chou seems to advocate is not escapism, but an attempt to harmonize with Lao-tzu's Taoist teaching on tact: "Is it empty talk, the old saying that tact keeps you whole? When truthfulness is complete, it still resorts to this" (*Tao Te Ching* 22). Because Chuang Chou was concerned with both spiritual and social liberty, Lao-tzu and Confucius are important figures in his symbolic stories.

Chuang Chou's approach to freedom was psychological and social as well as political. He encouraged people to seek freedom from tyranny and oppression of all kinds, whether political, social, intellectual, or emotional. He even inspired people to seek liberation from the ultimate tyranny of death. As a philosopher and as a man, Chuang Chou had the audacity to lay bare the root of the human condition; having set aside his illusions, he could not be manipulated by either hope or fear.

Chuang-tzu, the book of Chuang Chou, consists of three sections, known as the inner, outer, and miscellaneous chapters. The inner chapters are the first seven, attributed to Chuang Chou himself and containing the essence of the teachings. This volume on the essential Tao presents an original translation of that basic core, the inner chapters of *Chuang-tzu,* with notes outlining the philosophy and symbolism of this classic work.

Tao Te Ching

1. A Way Can Be a Guide

A way can be a guide, but not a fixed path;
names can be given, but not permanent labels.
Nonbeing is called the beginning of heaven and
    earth;
being is called the mother of all things.
Always passionless, thereby observe the subtle;
ever intent, thereby observe the apparent.
These two come from the same source but differ in
    name;
both are considered mysteries.
The mystery of mysteries
is the gateway of marvels.

2. Everyone Knows

When everyone knows beauty is beauty,
this is bad.
When everyone knows good is good,
this is not good.
So being and nonbeing produce each other:
difficulty and ease complement each other,
long and short shape each other,
high and low contrast with each other,
voice and echoes conform to each other,
before and after go along with each other.
So sages manage effortless service
and carry out unspoken guidance.
All beings work, without exception:
if they live without possessiveness,
act without presumption,
and do not dwell on success,
then by this very nondwelling
success will not leave.

3. *Not Exalting Cleverness*

Not exalting cleverness
causes the people not to contend.
Not putting high prices on hard-to-get goods
causes the people not to steal.
Not seeing anything to want
causes the mind not to be confused.
Therefore the government of sages
empties the mind and fills the middle,
weakens the ambition and strengthens the bones,
always keeping the people innocent and
      passionless.
It makes the sophisticated not dare to contrive;
action being without contrivance,
nothing is disordered.

4. *The Way Is Unimpeded Harmony*

The Way is unimpeded harmony;
its potential may never be fully exploited.
It is as deep as the source of all things:
it blunts the edges,
resolves the complications,
harmonizes the light,
assimilates to the world.
Profoundly still, it seems to be there:
I don't know whose child it is,
before the creation of images.

5. *Heaven and Earth*

Heaven and earth are not humane;
they regard all beings as straw dogs.
Sages are not humane;
they see all people as straw dogs.
The space between heaven and earth
is like bellows and pipes,
empty yet inexhaustible,
producing more with movement.
The talkative reach their wits' end
again and again;
that is not as good as keeping centered.

6. *The Valley Spirit*

The valley spirit not dying
is called the mysterious female.
The opening of the mysterious female
is called the root of heaven and earth.
Continuous, on the brink of existence,
to put it into practice, don't try to force it.

7. *Heaven Is Eternal, Earth Is Everlasting*

Heaven is eternal, earth is everlasting.
The reason they can be eternal and everlasting
is that they do not foster themselves;
that is why they can live forever.
For this reason sages put themselves last,
and they were first;
they excluded themselves,
and they survived.
Was it not by their very selflessness
that they managed to fulfill themselves?

8. *Higher Good Is like Water*

Higher good is like water:
the good in water benefits all,
and does so without contention.
It rests where people dislike to be,
so it is close to the Way.
Where it dwells becomes good ground;
profound is the good in its heart,
benevolent the good it bestows.
Goodness in words is trustworthiness,
goodness in government is order;
goodness in work is ability,
goodness in action is timeliness.
But only by noncontention
is there nothing extreme.

9. To Keep on Filling

To keep on filling
is not as good as stopping.
Calculated sharpness
cannot be kept for long.
Though gold and jewels fill their houses,
no one can keep them.
When the rich upper classes are haughty,
their legacy indicts them.
When one's work is accomplished honorably,
to retire is the Way of heaven.

10. Carrying Vitality and Consciousness

Carrying vitality and consciousness,
embracing them as one,
can you keep them from parting?
Concentrating energy,
making it supple,
can you be like an infant?
Purifying hidden perception,
can you make it flawless?
Loving the people, governing the nation,
can you be uncontrived?
As the gate of heaven opens and closes,
can you be impassive?
As understanding reaches everywhere,
can you be innocent?
Producing and developing,
producing without possessing,
doing without presuming,
growing without domineering:
this is called mysterious power.

11. *Thirty Spokes*

Thirty spokes join at the hub:
their use for the cart
is where they are not.
When the potter's wheel makes a pot,
the use of the pot
is precisely where there is nothing.
When you open doors and windows for a room,
it is where there is nothing
that they are useful to the room.
Therefore being is for benefit,
Nonbeing is for usefulness.

12. *Colors*

Colors blind people's eyes,
sounds deafen their ears;
flavors spoil people's palates,
the chase and the hunt
craze people's minds;
goods hard to obtain
make people's actions harmful.
Therefore sages work for the middle
and not the eyes,
leaving the latter and taking the former.

13. *Favor and Disgrace*

Favor and disgrace seem alarming;
high status greatly afflicts your person.
What are favor and disgrace?
Favor is the lower:
get it and you're surprised,
lose it and you're startled.
This means favor and disgrace are alarming.
Why does high status greatly afflict your person?
The reason we have a lot of trouble
is that we have selves.
If we had no selves,
what troubles would we have?
Therefore those who embody nobility
to act for the sake of the world
seem to be able to draw the world to them,
while those who embody love
to act for the sake of the world
seem to be worthy of the trust of the world.

14. *When You Look at It You Don't See It*

What you don't see when you look
is called the unobtrusive.
What you don't hear when you listen
is called the rarefied.
What you don't get when you grasp
is called the subtle.
These three cannot be completely fathomed,
so they merge into one;
above is not bright, below is not dark.
Continuous, unnameable, it returns again to
     nothing.
This is called the stateless state,
the image of no thing;
this is called mental abstraction.
When you face it you do not see its head,
when you follow it you do not see its back.
Hold the ancient Way
so as to direct present existence:
only when you can know the ancient
can this be called the basic cycle of the Way.

Skilled warriors of old were subtle,
mysteriously powerful,
so deep they were unknowable.
Just because they are unknowable,
I will try to describe them.
Their wariness was as that of one crossing a river
    in winter,
their caution was as that of one in fear of all
    around;
their gravity was as that of a guest,
their relaxation was as that of ice at the melting
    point.
Simple as uncarved wood,
open as the valleys,
they were inscrutable as murky water.
Who can, in turbidity,
use the gradual clarification of stillness?
Who can, long at rest,
use the gradual enlivening of movement?
Those who preserve this Way do not want fullness.
Just because of not wanting fullness,
it is possible to use to the full and not make anew.

16. *Attain the Climax of Emptiness*

Attain the climax of emptiness,
preserve the utmost quiet:
as myriad things act in concert,
I thereby observe the return.
Things flourish,
then each returns to its root.
Returning to the root is called stillness:
stillness is called return to Life,
return to Life is called the constant;
knowing the constant is called enlightenment.
Acts at random, in ignorance of the constant, bode
    ill.
Knowing the constant gives perspective;
this perspective is impartial.
Impartiality is the highest nobility;
the highest nobility is divine,
and the divine is the Way.
This Way is everlasting,
not endangered by physical death.

17. *Very Great Leaders*

Very great leaders in their domains
are only known to exist.
Those next best are beloved and praised.
The lesser are feared and despised.
Therefore when faith is insufficient
and there is disbelief,
it is from the high value placed on words.
Works are accomplished, tasks are completed,
and ordinary folk all say
they are acting spontaneously.

---

18. *When the Great Way Is Deserted*

When the Great Way is deserted,
then there is humanitarian duty.
When intelligence comes forth,
there is great fabrication.
When relations are discordant,
then there is family love.
When the national polity
is benighted and confused,
then there are loyal ministers.

19. *Eliminate Sagacity, Abandon Knowledge*

Eliminate sagacity, abandon knowledge,
and the people benefit a hundredfold.
Eliminate humanitarianism, abandon duty,
and the people return to familial love.
Eliminate craft, abandon profit,
and theft will no longer exist.
These three become insufficient
when used for embellishment
causing there to be attachments.
See the basic,
embrace the unspoiled,
lessen selfishness,
diminish desire.

20. *Detach from Learning and You Have No Worries*

Detach from learning and you have no worries.
How far apart are yes and yeah?
How far apart are good and bad?
The things people fear cannot but be feared.
Wild indeed the uncentered!
Most people celebrate
as if they were barbecuing a slaughtered cow,
or taking in the springtime vistas;
I alone am aloof,
showing no sign,
like an infant that doesn't yet smile,
riding buoyantly
as if with nowhere to go.
Most people have too much;
I alone seem to be missing something.
Mine is indeed the mind of an ignoramus
in its unadulterated simplicity.
Ordinary people try to shine;
I alone seem to be dark.
Ordinary people try to be on the alert;
I alone am unobtrusive,
calm as the ocean depths,
buoyant as if anchored nowhere.
Most people have ways and means;
I alone am unsophisticated and simple.
I alone am different from people
in that I value seeking food from the mother.

21. *The Countenance of Great Virtue*

For the countenance of great virtue,
only the Way is to be followed.
As a thing, the Way is abstract and elusive:
elusive and abstract, there are images in it;
abstract and elusive, there is something there.
Recondite, hidden, it has vitality therein:
that vitality is very real;
it has truth therein.
From ancient times to now,
its name is the undeparting;
thereby are seen all beauties.
How do I know all beauties are thus?
By this.

Be tactful and you remain whole;
bend and you remain straight.
The hollow is filled,
the old is renewed.
Economy is gain,
excess is confusion.
Therefore sages embrace unity
as a model for the world.
Not seeing themselves,
they are therefore clear.
Not asserting themselves,
they are therefore outstanding.
Not congratulating themselves,
they are therefore meritorious.
Not taking pride in themselves,
they last long.
It is just because they do not contend
that no one in the world can contend with them.
Is it empty talk, the old saying
that tact keeps you whole?
When truthfulness is complete,
it still resorts to this.

23. To Speak Rarely Is Natural

To speak rarely is natural.
That is why a gusty wind doesn't last the morning,
a downpour of rain doesn't last the day.
Who does this? Heaven and earth.
If even heaven and earth cannot go on forever,
how much less can human beings!
Therefore those who follow the Way assimilate to
     the Way;
the virtuous assimilate to virtue,
those who have lost assimilate to loss.
Those who assimilate to the Way are happy to
     gain it,
those who assimilate to virtue too are happy to
     gain it,
and those who assimilate to loss are also happy to
     gain it.
When trust is insufficient, there is distrust.

24. Those on Tiptoe Don't Stand Up

Those on tiptoe don't stand up,
those who take long strides don't walk;
those who see themselves are not perceptive,
those who assert themselves are not illustrious;
those who glorify themselves have no merit,
those who are proud of themselves do not last.
On the Way, these are called overconsumption
and excess activity.
Some people disdain them,
so those with the Way abstain.

25. *Something Undifferentiated*

Something undifferentiated was born before heaven
        and earth;
still and silent, standing alone and unchanging,
going through cycles unending,
able to be mother to the world.
I do not know its name;
I label it the Way.
Imposing on it a name,
I call it Great.
Greatness means it goes;
going means reaching afar;
reaching afar means return.
Therefore the Way is great,
heaven is great,
earth is great,
and kingship is also great.
Among domains are four greats,
of which kingship is one.
Humanity emulates earth,
earth emulates heaven,
heaven emulates the Way,
the Way emulates Nature.

26. *Gravity Is the Root of Lightness*

Gravity is the root of lightness;
calm is the master of excitement.
Thereby do exemplary people travel all day
without leaving their equipment.
Though they have a look of prosperity,

24

their resting place is transcendent.
What can be done about heads of state
who take the world lightly in their own self-
        interest?
Lack of gravity loses servants of state;
instability loses heads of state.

27.   *Good Works*

Good works are trackless,
good words are flawless,
good planning isn't calculating.
What is well closed has no bolt locking it,
but cannot be opened.
What is well bound has no rope confining it,
but cannot be untied.
Therefore sages always consider it good to save
        people,
so that there are no wasted humans;
they always consider it good to save beings,
so that there are no wasted beings.
So good people are teachers
of people who are not good.
People who are not good
are students of people who are good.
Those who do not honor teachers or care for
        students
are greatly deluded, even if knowledgeable.
This is called an essential subtlety.

28. *Know the Male*

Know the male, keep the female;
be humble toward the world.
Be humble to the world,
and eternal power never leaves,
returning again to innocence.
Knowing the white, keep the black;
be an exemplar for the world.
Be an exemplar for the world,
and eternal power never goes awry,
returning again to infinity.
Knowing the glorious, keep the ignominious;
be open to the world.
Be open to the world,
and eternal power suffices,
returning again to simplicity.
Simplicity is lost to make instruments,
which sages employ as functionaries.
Therefore the great fashioner does no splitting.

29. *Should You Want*

Should you want to take the world,
and contrive to do so,
I see you won't manage to finish.
The most sublime instrument in the world
cannot be contrived.
Those who contrive spoil it;
those who cling lose it.

So creatures sometimes go and sometimes follow,
sometimes puff and sometimes blow,
are sometimes strong and sometimes weak,
begin sometime and end sometime;
therefore sages remove extremes,
remove extravagance,
remove arrogance.

30. *Assisting Human Leaders with the Way*

Those who assist human leaders with the Way
do not coerce the world with weapons,
for these things are apt to backfire.
Brambles grow where an army has been;
there are always bad years after a war.
Therefore the good are effective, that is all;
they do not presume to grab power thereby:
they are effective but not conceited,
effective but not proud,
effective but not arrogant.
They are effective when they have to be,
effective but not coercive.
If you peak in strength, you then age;
this, it is said, is unguided.
The unguided soon come to an end.

Fine weapons are implements of ill omen:
people may despise them,
so those with the Way do not dwell with them.
Therefore the place of honor for the cultured is on
    the left,
while the honored place for the martialist is on the
    right.
Weapons, being instruments of ill omen,
are not the tools of the cultured,
who use them only when unavoidable.
They consider it best to be aloof;
they win without beautifying it.
Those who beautify it
enjoy killing people.
Those who enjoy killing
cannot get their will of the world.
The left is favored for auspicious things,
the right for things of ill omen:
so the subordinate general is on the left,
the top general on the right.
That means when you are in ascendancy of power
you handle it as you would a mourning.
When you have killed many people,
you weep for them in sorrow.
When you win a war,
you celebrate by mourning.

32. *The Way Is Eternally Nameless*

The Way is eternally nameless.
Though simplicity is small,
the world cannot subordinate it.
If lords and monarchs can keep to it,
all beings will naturally resort to them.
Heaven and earth combine,
thus showering sweet dew.
No humans command it;
it is even by nature.
Start fashioning, and there are names;
once names also exist,
you should know when to stop.
By knowing when to stop,
you are not endangered.
The Way is to the world
as rivers and oceans to valley streams.

33. *Those Who Know Others*

Those who know others are wise;
those who know themselves are enlightened.
Those who overcome others are powerful;
those who overcome themselves are strong.
Those who are contented are rich;
those who act strongly have will.
Those who do not lose their place endure;
those who die without perishing live long.

34. The Great Way Is Universal

The Great Way is universal;
it can apply to the left or the right.
All beings depend on it for life,
and it does not refuse.
Its accomplishments fulfilled,
it does not dwell on them.
It lovingly nurtures all beings,
but does not act as their ruler.
As it has no desire, it can be called small.
As all beings take to it,
yet it does not act as their ruler,
it can be called great.
Therefore sages never contrive greatness;
that is why they can become so great.

35. Holding the Great Image

When holding the Great Image,
the world goes on and on without harm,
peaceful, even, tranquil.
Where there is music and dining,
passing travelers stop;
but the issue of the Way
is so plain as to be flavorless.
When you look at it, it is invisible;
when you listen to it, it is inaudible;
when you use it, it cannot be exhausted.

36. *Should You Want to Contain*

Should you want to contain something,
you must deliberately let it expand.
Should you want to weaken something,
you must deliberately let it grow strong.
Should you want to eliminate something,
you must deliberately allow it to flourish.
Should you want to take something away,
you must deliberately grant it.
This is called subtle illumination.
Flexibility and yielding
overcome adamant coerciveness.
Fish shouldn't be taken from the depths;
the effective tools of the nation
shouldn't be shown to others.

37. *The Way Is Always Uncontrived*

The Way is always uncontrived,
yet there's nothing it doesn't do.
If lords and monarchs could keep to it,
all beings would evolve spontaneously.
When they have evolved and want to act,
I would stabilize them with nameless simplicity.
Even nameless simplicity would not be wanted.
By not wanting, there is calm,
and the world will straighten itself.

38. *Higher Virtue Is Not Ingratiating*

Higher virtue is not ingratiating;
that is why it has virtue.
Lower virtue does not forget about reward;
that is why it is virtueless.
Higher virtue is uncontrived,
and there is no way to contrive it.
Lower virtue is created,
and there is a way to do it.
Higher humanity is created,
but there is no way to contrive it.
Higher duty is done,
and there is a way to do it.
Higher courtesy is done,
but no one responds to it;
so there is forceful repetition.
Therefore virtue comes after loss of the Way;
humanity comes after loss of virtue,
duty comes after loss of humanity,
courtesy comes after loss of duty.
Manners mean loyalty and trust are thin,
and disarray's beginning.
Foresight is a flower of the Way,
and the beginning of ignorance too.
Therefore great people dwell in the thick,
not the thin.
They abide in the substance,
not the flower.
So they leave the latter and take the former.

When unity was attained of old,
heaven became clear by attaining unity,
earth became steady by attaining unity,
spirit was quickened by attaining unity,
valley streams were filled by attaining unity,
all beings were born by attaining unity;
and by attaining unity lords acted rightly
for the sake of the world.
What brought this about was unity:
without means of clarity, heaven may burst;
without means of steadiness, earth may erupt;
without means of quickening, spirit may be
        exhausted;
without means of filling, valley streams may dry
        up;
without means of birth, all beings may perish;
without means of acting rightly, lords may
        stumble.
Therefore nobility is rooted in humility,
loftiness is based on lowliness.
This is why noble people refer to themselves
as alone, lacking, and unworthy.
Is this not being rooted in humility?
So there is no praise in repeated praise;
they don't want to be like jewels or like stones.

40. *Return Is the Movement of the Way*

Return is the movement of the Way;
yielding is the function of the Way.
All things in the world are born of being;
being is born of nonbeing.

41. *When Superior People Hear of the Way*

When superior people hear of the Way,
they carry it out with diligence.
When middling people hear of the Way,
it sometimes seems to be there, sometimes not.
When lesser people hear of the Way,
they ridicule it greatly.
If they didn't laugh at it,
it wouldn't be the Way.
So there are constructive sayings on this:
The Way of illumination seems dark,
the Way of advancement seems retiring,
the Way of equality seems to categorize;
higher virtue seems empty,
great purity seems ignominious,
broad virtue seems insufficient,
constructive virtue seems careless.
Simple honesty seems changeable,
great range has no boundaries,
great vessels are finished late;
the great sound has a rarefied tone,
the great image has no form,
the Way hides in namelessness.
Only the Way can enhance and perfect.

42. The Way Produces One

The Way produces one;
one produces two,
two produce three,
three produce all beings:
all beings bear yin and embrace yang,
with a mellowing energy for harmony.
The things people dislike
are only to be alone, lacking, and unworthy;
yet these are what monarchs call themselves.
Therefore people may gain from loss,
and may lose from gain.
What others teach,
I also teach.
The strong cannot master their death:
I take this to be the father of teachings.

43. What Is Softest in the World

What is softest in the world
drives what is hardest in the world.
Nonbeing enters where there is no room;
that is how we know noncontrivance enhances.
Unspoken guidance and uncontrived enhancement
are reached by few in the world.

44. *Name or Body*

Which is closer, your name or your body?
Which is more, your body or your possessions?
Which is more destructive, gain or loss?
Extreme fondness means great expense,
and abundant possessions mean much loss.
If you know when you have enough,
you will not be disgraced.
If you know when to stop,
you will not be endangered.
It is possible thereby to live long.

45. *Great Completeness Seems Incomplete*

Great completeness seems incomplete;
its use is never exhausted.
Great fullness seems empty;
its use is never ended.
Great directness seems restrained,
great skill seems inept,
great eloquence seems inarticulate.
Movement overcomes cold,
stillness overcomes heat.
Clear stillness is right for the world.

46. *When the World Has the Way*

When the world has the Way,
running horses are retired to till the fields.
When the world lacks the Way,
war-horses are bred in the countryside.
No crime is greater than approving of greed;
no calamity is greater than discontent,
no fault is greater than possessiveness.
So the satisfaction of contentment is always
     enough.

47. *Without Even Going out the Door*

They know the world
without even going out the door.
They see the sky and its pattern
without even looking out the window.
The further out it goes, the less knowledge is;
therefore sages know without going,
name without seeing,
complete without striving.

48. *For Learning You Gain Daily*

For learning you gain daily;
for the Way you lose daily.
Losing and losing,
thus you reach noncontrivance;
be uncontrived, and nothing is not done.
Taking the world is always done
by not making anything of it.
For when something is made of it,
that is not enough to take the world.

49. *Sages Have No Fixed Mind*

Sages have no fixed mind;
they make the minds of the people their mind:
they improve the good,
and also improve those who are not good;
that virtue is good.
They make sure of the true,
and they make sure of the untrue too;
that virtue is sure.
The relation of sages to the world
is one of concern:
they cloud their minds for the world;
all people pour into their ears and eyes,
and sages render them innocent.

Exiting life, we enter death.
The followers of life are three out of ten,
the followers of death are three out of ten;
in the lives of the people,
the dying grounds on which they are agitated
are also three out of ten.
What is the reason?
Because of the seriousness
with which they take life as life.
It has been said
that those who maintain life well
do not meet rhinos or tigers on land
and do not arm themselves in war.
There is no way for rhinos to gore them;
there is no way for tigers to claw them;
there is no way for weapons to get at them.
Why? Because they have no dying ground.

51. *The Way Gives Birth*

The Way gives birth,
virtue nurtures,
things form,
momentum completes.
Therefore all beings honor the Way
and value its Virtue.
The honor of the Way
and the value of Virtue
are not granted by anyone,
but are always naturally so.
So the Way gives birth and nurtures,
makes grow and develops,
completes and matures,
builds up and breaks down.
It produces but does not possess;
it acts without presumption,
it fosters growth without ruling.
This is called hidden Virtue.

52. *The World Has a Beginning*

The world has a beginning
that is the mother of the world.
Once you've found the mother,
thereby you know the child.
Once you know the child,
you return to keep the mother,
not perishing though the body die.
Close your eyes, shut your doors,

and you do not toil all your life.
Open your eyes, carry out your affairs,
and you are not saved all your life.
Seeing the small is called clarity;
keeping flexible is called strength.
Using the shining radiance,
you return again to the light,
not leaving anything to harm yourself.
This is called entering the eternal.

53.   *Causing One Flashes*

Causing one flashes of knowledge
to travel the Great Way,
only its application demands care.
The Great Way is quite even,
yet people prefer byways.
When courts are extremely fastidious,
the fields are seriously neglected,
and the granaries are very empty;
they wear colorful clothing
and carry sharp swords,
eat and drink to their fill
and possess more than enough.
This is called the vanity of thieves;
it is not the Way.

54. *Good Construction Does Not Fall Down*

Good construction does not fall down,
a good embrace does not let go;
their heirs honor them unceasingly.
Cultivate it in yourself, and that virtue is real;
cultivate it in the home, and that virtue is
     abundant;
cultivate it in the locality, and that virtue lasts;
cultivate it in the nation, and that virtue is rich;
cultivate it in the world, and that virtue is
     universal.
So observe yourself by yourself,
observe the home by the home,
observe the locality by the locality,
observe the nation by the nation,
observe the world by the world.
How do I know the world is as it is?
By this.

55. *The Richness of Subliminal Virtue*

The richness of subliminal virtue
is comparable to an infant:
poisonous creatures do not sting it,
wild beasts do not claw it,
predatory birds do not grab it.
Its tendons are flexible,
yet its grip is firm.
Even while it knows not of the mating of male and
     female,
its genitals get aroused;

this is the epitome of vitality.
It can cry all day without choking or getting
     hoarse;
this is the epitome of harmony.
Knowing harmony is called constancy,
knowing constancy is called clarity;
enhancing life is called propitious,
the mind mastering energy is called strong.
When beings climax in power, they wane;
this is called being unguided.
The unguided die early.

56.   *Those Who Know Do Not Say*

Those who know do not say;
those who say do not know.
Close the senses,
shut the doors;
blunt the sharpness,
resolve the complications;
harmonize the light,
assimilate to the world.
This is called mysterious sameness.
It cannot be made familiar,
yet cannot be estranged;
it cannot be profited,
yet cannot be harmed;
it cannot be valued,
yet cannot be demeaned.
Therefore it is precious for the world.

57. *Govern Nations by Normalcy*

Use straightforwardness for civil government,
use surprise for military operations;
use noninvolvement to take the world.
How do I know this?
The more taboos there are in the world,
the poorer the populace is;
the more crafts the people have,
the more exotic things are produced;
the more laws are promulgated,
the greater the number of thieves.
Therefore the sage says,
I contrive nothing,
and the people are naturally civilized;
I am fond of tranquility,
and the people are naturally upright.
I have nothing to do,
and the people are naturally enriched;
I have no desire,
and the people are naturally simple.

58. *When the Government Is Unobtrusive*

When the government is unobtrusive,
the people are pure.
When the government is invasive,
the people are wanting.
Calamity is what fortune depends upon;
fortune is what calamity subdues.
Who knows how it will all end?

Is there no right and wrong?
The orthodox also becomes unorthodox,
the good also becomes ill;
people's confusion
is indeed long-standing.
Therefore sages are upright without causing injury,
honest without hurting,
direct but not tactless,
illumined but not flashy.

59.   *To Govern the Human and Serve the Divine*

To govern the human and serve the divine,
nothing compares to frugality.
Only frugality brings early recovery;
early recovery means buildup of power.
Build up virtue,
and you master all.
When you master all,
no one knows your limit.
When no one knows your limit,
you can maintain a nation.
When you maintain the matrix of a nation,
you can last long.
This is called making the root deep and the basis
      firm,
the Way of long life and eternal vision.

60. *Governing a Large Nation Is like Cooking Small Fry*

Governing a large nation
is like cooking little fish.
When the world is ruled by the Way,
the ghosts are powerless.
It is not that the ghosts are powerless;
their spirits do not harm the people.
Not only do the spirits not harm the people;
sages do not harm the people either.
Because the two do not harm each other,
their virtues ultimately combine.

61. *A Great Nation Flows Downward*

A great nation flows downward
into intercourse with the world.
The female of the world
always prevails over the male by stillness.
Because stillness is considered lower,
by lowering itself to a small nation
a great nation takes a small nation;
by being lower than a great nation
a small nation takes a great nation.
So one takes by lowering itself,
another takes by being lower.
A great nation wants no more
than to include and nurture people;
a small nation wants no more
than to admit and serve people.
Both get what they want,
so the great should be below.

62. *The Way Is the Pivot of All Things*

The Way is the pivot of all things:
the treasure of good people,
the safeguard of those who are not good.
Fine words can be sold,
honored acts can oppress people;
why should people who are not good abandon
     them?
Therefore to establish an emperor
and set up high officials,
one may have a great jewel
and drive a team of horses,
but that is not as good
as advancing calmly on this Way.
Why did the ancients value this Way?
By it one can attain without long seeking
and escape from the faults one has;
therefore it is valued by the world.

63.   *Do Nondoing*

Do nondoing,
strive for nonstriving,
savor the flavorless,
regard the small as important,
make much of little,
repay enmity with virtue;
plan for difficulty when it is still easy,
do the great while it is still small.
The most difficult things in the world
must be done while they are easy;
the greatest things in the world
must be done while they are small.
Because of this sages never do great things;
that is why they can fulfill their greatness.
If you agree too easily, you'll be little trusted;
if you take it easy a lot, you'll have a lot of
        problems.
Therefore it is through difficulty
that sages end up without problems.

64.   *What Is at Rest Is Easy to Hold*

What is at rest
is easy to hold.
What has not shown up
is easy to take into account.
What is frail
is easy to break.
What is vague
is easy to dispel.

Do it before it exists;
govern it before there's disorder.
The most massive tree grows from a sprout;
the highest building rises from a pile of earth;
a journey of a thousand miles begins with a step.
Those who contrive spoil it;
those who cling lose it.

Thus sages contrive nothing,
and so spoil nothing.
They cling to nothing,
and so lose nothing.

Therefore people's works
are always spoiled on the verge of completion.
Be as careful of the end
as of the beginning,
and nothing will be spoiled.

Thus sages want to have no wants;
they do not value goods hard to get.
They learn not learning
to recover from people's excesses,
thereby to assist
the naturalness of all beings,
without daring to contrive.

65.   *Good Practitioners of the Way in Ancient Times*

In ancient times,
good practitioners of the Way
did not use it to enlighten the people,
but to make them unsophisticated.

When people are unruly,
it is because of their sophistication.
So to govern a country by cunning
is to rob the country.
Not using cunning to govern a country
is good fortune for the country.
To know these two
is also a model.
Being always aware of the model
is called hidden virtue.

Hidden virtue is deep, far-reaching,
in contrast to ordinary people.
Only when it is thus
does it reach great accord.

66.   *Rivers and Seas Are Lords of the Hundred Valleys*

The reason why rivers and seas
can be lords of the hundred valleys
is that they lower themselves to them well;
therefore they can be lords
of the hundred valleys.
So when sages wish to rise above people,
they lower themselves to them in their speech.
When they want to precede people,
they go after them in status.
So when sages rule,
people don't take it gravely.
And when sages are in the forefront,
people don't attack them.
Therefore the world happily backs them
and does not tire of them.
Because they do not contend,
no one in the world can contend with them.

67. *Everyone Says*

Everyone in the world
says my Way is great,
but it seems incomparable.
It is just because it is great
that it seems incomparable:
when comparisons are long established
it becomes trivialized.

I have three treasures
that I keep and hold:
one is mercy,
the second is frugality,
the third is not presuming
to be at the head of the world.
By reason of mercy,
one can be brave.
By reason of frugality,
one can be broad.
By not presuming
to be at the head of the world,
one can make your potential last.

Now if one were bold
but had no mercy,
if one were broad
but were not frugal,
if one went ahead
without deference,
one would die.

Use mercy in war,
and you win;
use it for defense,
and you're secure.
Those whom heaven is going to save
are those it guards with mercy.

68.   *Good Warriors*

Good warriors do not arm,
good fighters don't get mad,
good winners don't contend,
good employers serve their workers.
This is called the virtue
of noncontention;
this is called mating with
the supremely natural and pristine.

69. *Sayings on Military Operations*

There are sayings on the use of arms:
"Let us not be aggressors,
but defend."
"Let us not advance an inch,
but retreat a foot."
This is called carrying out no action,
shaking no arm,
facing no enemy,
wielding no weapon.
No calamity is greater
than underestimating opponents.
If you underestimate opponents,
you're close to losing your treasure.
So when opposing armies clash,
the compassionate
are the ones who win.

70. *My Sayings Are Very Easy to Recognize*

My sayings are very easy to recognize,
and very easy to apply.
But no one in the world can recognize them,
and no one can apply them.
Sayings have a source,
events have a leader.
It is only through ignorance
that I am not known.
Those who know me are rare;
those who emulate me are noble.
This is why sages dress plainly,
and conceal what is precious.

71.   *Knowing Unconsciously*

To know unconsciously is best.
To presume to know what you don't
is sick.
Only by recognizing the sickness
of sickness
is it possible not to be sick.
The sages' freedom from ills
was from recognizing the sickness of sickness,
so they didn't suffer from sickness.

72.   *When the People Are Not Awed by Authority*

When the people are not awed by authority,
then great authority is attained.
Their homes are not small to them,
their livelihood not tiresome.
Just because they do not tire of it,
it is not tiresome to them.

Therefore sages know themselves
but do not see themselves.
They take care of themselves
but do not exalt themselves.
So they take one
and leave the other.

73. *Boldness in Daring Means Killing*

Boldness in daring means killing;
boldness in not daring means life.
These two may help and may harm.
Who knows the reason
for what heaven dislikes?
This is why even sages
find it hard for them.
The Way of heaven
wins well without contest,
responds well without speech,
comes of itself uncalled,
relaxed yet very resourceful.
The net of heaven is vast;
the holes are large
but don't let slip.

74. *If People Usually Don't Fear Death*

If people usually don't fear death,
how can death be used to scare them?
If people are made to fear death,
and you can catch and kill them
when they act oddly,
who would dare?

There are always executioners.
And to kill in place of an executioner
is taking the place
of a master carver.
Those who take the place
of a master carver
rarely avoid cutting their hands.

75. *People's Starvation*

When people are starving,
it is because their governments take too much,
causing them to starve.
When people are hard to control,
it is because of the contrivances of their
        governments,
which make them hard to control.
When people slight death,
it is because of the earnestness
with which they seek life;
that makes them slight death.
Only those who do not contrive to live
are wise in valuing life.

76. *When People Are Born*

When people are born they are supple,
and when they die they are stiff.
When trees are born they are tender,
and when they die they are brittle.
Stiffness is thus a companion of death,
flexibility a companion of life.
So when an army is strong,
it does not prevail.
When a tree is strong,
it is cut for use.
So the stiff and strong are below,
the supple and yielding on top.

77. The Way of Heaven

The Way of heaven
is like drawing a bow:
the high is lowered,
the low is raised;
excess is reduced,
need is fulfilled.
The Way of heaven
reduces excess and fills need,
but the way of humans is not so:
they strip the needy
to serve those who have too much.

78. The Most Flexible Thing in the World

Nothing in the world is more flexible
and yielding than water.
Yet when it attacks the firm and the strong,
none can withstand it,
because they have no way to change it.
So the flexible overcome the adamant,
the yielding overcome the forceful.
Everyone knows this,
but no one can do it.
This is why sages say
those who can take on the disgrace of nations
are leaders of lands;
those who can take on the misfortune of nations
are rulers of the world.
True sayings seem paradoxical.

79. *Harmonize Bitter Enemies*

When you harmonize bitter enemies,
yet resentment is sure to linger,
how can this be called good?
Therefore sages keep their faith
and do not pressure others.
So the virtuous see to their promises,
while the virtueless look after precedents.
The Way of heaven is impersonal;
it is always with good people.

80. *A Small State Has Few People*

A small state has few people.
It has the people keep arms
but not use them.
It has them regard death gravely
and not go on distant campaigns.
Even if they have vehicles,
they have nowhere to drive them.
Even if they have weapons,
they have nowhere to use them.
It has the people go back to simple techniques,
relish their food,
like their clothes,
be comfortable in their ways,
and enjoy their work.
Neighboring states may be so close
they can hear each other's dogs and roosters,
but they make it so that the people
have never gone back and forth.

81. *True Words Are Not Beautiful*

True words are not beautiful,
beautiful words are not true.
The good are not argumentative,
the argumentative are not good.
Knowers do not generalize,
generalists do not know.
Sages do not accumulate anything
but give everything to others,
having more the more they give.
The Way of heaven
helps and does not harm.
The Way for humans
is to act without contention.

Chuang-tzu

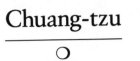

1

Freedom

In the Northern Deep there is a great fish, thousands of miles long. It turns into a giant bird whose back is thousands of miles in size. When it gets aroused and takes to flight, its wings are like clouds covering the sky.

When the ocean rolls, this bird sets off for the Southern Deep, which is the Pond of Heaven. A chronicler of unusual phenomena writes, "When the giant bird moves to the Southern Deep, it beats on the water for three thousand miles, whipping up a whirlwind and taking off on it, rising ninety thousand miles. It comes to rest six months after leaving."

Energy is movement, particulate matter, the breathing of living beings in concert: is the blue of the sky its real color, or is it so far-reaching as to be endless? This is how things seem to the vision of the giant bird when it looks down.

Now if water has not accumulated to sufficient depth, it does not have the power to carry a large boat. Pour a cup of water into a depression, and a mustard seed will be as a boat in it; but put the cup into the water, and it will stay put, because the water is too shallow for the size of the boat.

If the air layer is not thick enough, it does not have the power to support the wings of the giant bird; therefore the bird rises ninety thousand miles, so that the wind is below it. Then it rides on the wind, its back to the clear empyrean, with nothing to get in its way; now it makes for the south.

The locust and the pigeon ridicule the giant bird, saying, "We rise up quickly into flight and aim for the trees. At that, sometimes we don't make it and land on the ground. Why go ninety thousand miles up to head for the south?"

Those who go into the bush come back after three meals with their bellies still full. Those who are going a hundred miles need overnight provisions. Those who are traveling a thousand miles need three months' supplies. So what do the locust and pigeon know? Small knowledge cannot reach great knowledge; those of little experience cannot comprehend those of great experience.

How do we know this is so? Morning mushrooms do not know the passing of days and nights, mayflies do not know the passing of spring and autumn. This is because they are short-lived.

In the south of Ch'u there is a tree for which spring was five hundred years and autumn five hundred years. In ancient times there was a great tree for which spring was eight thousand years and autumn was eight thousand years. And yet Grandfather P'eng [who is said to have lived for eight hundred years] is now noted for longevity. Are not ordinary people pitiful by comparison?

North of the desert there is a deep ocean, the Pond of Heaven. There is a fish in it that is thousands of miles wide and who knows how long. There is a bird there whose back is like an enormous mountain and whose wings are like clouds covering the sky. It grabs onto a whirlwind and rises ninety thousand miles, beyond the clouds, its back to the blue sky, and then makes for the south, going to the Southern Deep. Marsh quail ridicule it, saying, "Where is it going? We leap up no more than a few yards and fly around the reeds. This is as far as flight reaches; so where is that giant bird going?" This is the distinction between the small and the great.

So those whose knowledge is effective enough for one office, those whose conduct is compatible with one locality, those whose virtue is suitable for one ruler, and those who are sought for employment by one country look upon themselves in the same way as the marsh quail.

Thus the philosopher Jung of Sung laughed at them in derision; he was not encouraged even when everyone praised him, and he was not discouraged even when everyone denounced him. His determination of the division between inside and outside, his discernment of the boundary between glory and disgrace, only went this far. He was not occupied with the world, but even though he was thus, still he was not constructive.

Master Lieh rode on the wind, with serene expertise, returning after fifteen days. He was unconcerned with the acquisition of wealth, but though he avoided the need to walk, he still depended on something. If one can ride on the reality of heaven and earth, harnessing the expression of the six energies to travel through infinity, then what would one depend on?

Therefore complete people have no self, spiritual people have no merit, saintly people have no name.

○

When the ancient king Yao wanted to abdicate in favor of Hsü Yu, he said, "Why keep a torch burning when the sun and moon are out? Why go on irrigating when the seasonal rains are falling? If you were established, the world would be orderly; and yet I am still in charge of it. I see myself lacking, and ask you to run the country."

Hsü Yu said, "You are governing the country, and the country is already orderly. If I were to take over for you, would I be doing it for the name? Names are guests of realities; should I be a guest? A wild bird nesting in the deep forest needs no more than a single branch; a wild animal drinking from a river takes no more than its fill. Go home, Majesty! I have no use for the country. Even if the cook is not managing the kitchen, a priest does not step over the sacrificial offerings to take over for him."

○

Chien Wu said to Lien Shu, "I heard statements from Chieh Yü that are grandiose but have no point, going on without referring back. I was amazed at how his talk is endless as a river, very much out of the ordinary, remote from human sense."

Lien Shu asked, "What did he say?"

Chien Wu replied, "He said that there are spiritual people living on a certain mountain; their skin is like ice or snow, they are as delicate and graceful as virgins. They don't eat grain, but sip the wind and drink the dew. Mounted on the energy of the clouds, driving flying dragons, they travel beyond the four seas. Their spirits quiet, they prevent diseases and cause the yearly crops to ripen. I think this is crazy, and I don't believe it."

Lien Shu said, "Indeed, the blind have no way to see coloring, the deaf have no way to hear music. Blindness and deafness are not only physical conditions; they also exist in knowledge.

"These statements are like a maiden in bloom. As to the virtue of those people, they unite all beings into one. Society seeks when there is chaos, but who would go to all the trouble of national politics? Those people are invulnerable; they do not drown even in massive floods, they are not hot even in scorching droughts. The fact is that even their grime, their husk, could be used to mold the likes of great kings such as Yao and Shun. Who among them would willingly be concerned with things?"

o

Once a man of Sung went to the lands of Yueh selling hats. The people of Yueh, however, cut off their hair and tattooed their bodies; they had no use for the hats.

When Yao had established order among the people of the land and equalized government within the four seas, he went to see four philosophers and forgot about the world.

o

Hui-tzu said to Chuang-tzu, "The king of Wei gave me seeds of a giant gourd. I planted them and got a huge gourd. If I had filled it with water, it would not have been strong enough to be lifted, and if I had split it for a dipper it would have been too shallow to hold anything. It was certainly enormous, but I considered it useless and smashed it."

Chuang-tzu replied, "You are certainly inept when it comes to employing the great. There were people of Sung who were skilled at making a balm that prevented their hands from chapping; for generations they had worked as cotton bleachers. A traveler who had heard about this asked to buy the formula, offering a hundred pieces of gold.

"The clan of bleachers got together to discuss what to do. They said, 'We have been cotton bleachers for generations, earning no more than a few pieces of gold. Now we have a chance to make a hundred pieces of gold in one day. Let's give him the formula.'

"So the traveler got the formula for the balm. He used it to gain the pleasure of the king of Wu, who made him a general. Then when the men of Wu fought the men of Yueh in a battle on the water in winter, the men of Wu [who had the balm to prevent chapping] routed the men of Yueh. Now the king of Wu rewarded the man who had brought the balm formula by enfeoffing him as lord of his own domain.

"In either case, the ability to prevent chapping was the same, but there was a difference in the way it was employed: one man used it to be enfeoffed, the others were still cotton bleachers.

"Now suppose you have a huge gourd: why not make a coracle out of it and use it to sail on the rivers and lakes, instead of worrying about it being too shallow to hold anything? You are still confused, it seems."

Hui-tzu then said to Chuang-tzu, "I have a gigantic tree, but its trunk is too gnarled for the plumb line and its branches too twisted for the ruler: even if it were set in the middle of the road, carpenters would pay no attention to it. Now what you say is grandiose but useless, rejected by everyone alike."

Chuang-tzu replied, "Have you not seen a wildcat? It lowers itself close to the ground to watch for careless prey; it leaps this way and that, high and low, but then gets caught in a trap and dies. A yak, on the other hand, is enormous, it can do big things but cannot catch a rat. Now you have a huge tree and worry that it is useless: why not plant it in the vast plain of the homeland of Nothing Whatsoever, roaming in effortlessness by its side and sleeping in freedom beneath it? The reason it does not fall to the axe, and no one injures it, is that it cannot be exploited. So what's the trouble?"

2

On Equalizing Things

Tzu-ch'i of Nan-kuo sat leaning on an armrest. He looked up at the sky and sighed. It seemed that he was oblivious of his body and soul. Rising to stand before him, Yen-ch'eng Tzu-yu said, "What is your state? Is the body indeed to be made like a withered tree and the mind like dead ashes? The way you are leaning on the armrest now is not like before."

Tzu-ch'i said, "Is it not good that you have asked about this? Now I have forgotten myself. Do you recognize this?

"Even if you have heard the pipes of humanity, you have not heard the pipes of earth. Even if you have heard the pipes of earth, you have not heard the pipes of heaven."

Tzu-yu asked, "How is that done, may I ask?"

Tzu-ch'i said, "When the Great Mass exhales, that is called wind. It is not active now, but when it acts up, all openings howl furiously. Have you alone not heard its sound in the swaying of the mountain forests? The holes in a giant tree are like nose, mouth, and ears, like square boxes, like round cages, like mortars, like cavities, like depressions: some roar, some whistle, some chatter, some huff, some howl, some wail, some boom, some cry. Those that sing out first are followed by others chiming in; in a breeze there is a small concert, in a wind there is a grand concert. When the forceful wind stops, all the holes are empty. Do you alone not see the trees swaying?"

Tzu-yu said, "If those myriad holes are the pipes of the earth, and the pipes of humanity are the woodwind instruments, then may I ask what the pipes of heaven are?"

Tzu-ch'i said, "Their playing has myriad differences, and causes them to come from themselves. All partake on their own, but who is the motive force?"

O

Great knowledge is broad, small knowledge is petty. Great talk is powerful, small talk is loquacious.

O

In sleep, the soul communes; on waking, the body acts out. Mutual contact creates a pull, day by day struggling with the mind, slowly, deeply, insidiously.

O

Small fear is fearful, great fear is slow. In action they are like a bolt, an arrow, in their control over judgment. In stillness they are like a prayer, a pledge, in their attachment to victory. They kill like fall and winter, in the sense of daily dissolution. Their addiction to what they do is such as to be irreversible. Their satiation is like a seal, in that it disintegrates with age. The mind drawing near to death cannot bring about a restoration of positivity.

Joy, anger, sadness, happiness, worry, lament, vacillation, fearfulness, volatility, indulgence, licentiousness, pretentiousness—they are like music issuing from hollows, or moisture producing mildew. Day and night they interchange before us, yet no one knows where they sprout. Stop, stop! From morning to evening we find them; do they arise from the same source?

If not for other, there is no self. If not for self, nothing is apprehended. This is not remote, but we don't know what constitutes the cause. There seems to be a real director, but we cannot find any trace of it. Its effectiveness is already proven, but we don't see its form. It has sense, but no form.

The whole body is there with all its members, openings, and organs: with which is the self associated? Do you like any of them? That means you have selfishness therein. Then do all sometimes act as servants? As servants, are they incapable of taking care of one another? Do they alternate as ruler and subject? Evidently there is a real ruler existing therein: the matter of whether or not we gain a sense of it does not increase or decrease its reality.

Once we have taken on a definite form, we do not lose it until death. We oppose things, yet also follow them; we violate things, yet also submit to them: that activity is all like a galloping horse that no one can stop. Isn't it pitiful? We work all our lives without seeing it accomplish anything. We wearily work to exhaustion, without even knowing what it all goes back to. How can we not be sad about this? People may say at least it isn't death, but what help is that? As the physical constitution changes, so does the mind; how can this not be considered a great sorrow?

Is all human life benighted? Is it just that I alone am benighted, and there are others who are not benighted? As long as they follow their fixed mentalities as guides, who is alone and without guidance? Why should they substitute knowledge, when they have what their minds take for themselves? Even an ignoramus has some of that.

Even if the mind is not fixed, if there are judgments, this is "going today and arriving yesterday." This is how the nonexistent is taken to exist. If the nonexistent is taken to exist, even if there were spiritual leaders they wouldn't be capable of knowledge. What can I do about it myself?

Words are not just puffs of air; words carry something. But what they say is not definite, so is there actually something said? Or has there never been anything said? If they are different from a chick's cheeping, does that mean sounds have any meaning, or are they meaningless?

By what is the Way made obscure, so that there are truth and falsehood? By what are words made obscure, so that there are right and wrong? Where does the Way not exist? Where do words not apply?

The Way is made obscure by small achievements; words are made obscure by fancy rhetoric. This is why there are the judgments of the Confucians and Moists: because each affirms what the other denies and denies what the other affirms. If you want to affirm what they deny and deny what they affirm, nothing compares to using clarity.

There is nothing that is not a "that" and nothing that is not a "this." One does not see from the standpoint of another; knowing by oneself is knowing something. Therefore it is said, "'That' comes from 'this,' and 'this' is based on 'that.'" This explains how "that" and "this" arise simultaneously.

But when there is arising, there is passing away; and when there is passing away, there is arising. When there is right, there is wrong; when there is wrong, there is right. By affirming we deny; by denying we affirm.

Therefore sages do not go this way, but perceive it in the context of nature. This is also based on an affirmation.

A "this" is also a "that," and a "that" is also a "this." "That" is one judgment, and "this" is also one judgment. Ultimately, are there in fact "that" and "this," or are there no "that" or "this"? Nothing can be opposite to "that and this"—we call this fact the pivot of the Way. When the pivot is centered in its hub, thereby responding infinitely, then affirmation is one infinity, and negation is also one infinity.

That is why it is said, "Nothing compares to using clarity."

---
o

To use a finger to illustrate how "a 'finger' is not a finger" is not as good as using something other than a finger to illustrate how "a 'finger' is not a finger." To use a horse to show how "a 'horse' is not a horse" is not as good as using something other than a horse to show how "a 'horse' is not a horse."

Heaven and earth are one finger, myriad beings are one horse. Approving the appropriate and disapproving the inappropriate, a road is made by travel, things are affirmed by saying so; but how are they so? They are so insofar as they are affirmed. How are they not so? They are not so insofar as they are denied.

Beings inevitably affirm something, so they inevitably approve something. No one does not affirm, so no one does not approve.

For this reason, we may bring up the horizontal and the vertical, the ugly and the beautiful, the enormous, the suspicious, the deceitful, and the strange, and the Way comprehends all as one. When there is division, there is definition, but whatever is defined also disintegrates. Whenever there is no definition or disintegration, all things again are resolved into unity.

Only the enlightened know how to comprehend all as unity. Therefore they do not act except in the context of the totality. The totality is what works; work is efficiency, efficiency is attainment. When you reach attainment, you are near. It is just a matter of depending on this, which is so without our knowing why; this is called the Way.

○

To labor intellectually to make things one without knowing they are the same is called "three in the morning." What does "three in the morning" mean?

A man who raised monkeys said he would give them three chestnuts in the morning and four in the evening. The monkeys all became angry at this. Then the man said instead he would give them four in the morning and three in the evening. Now the monkeys were all happy. There was no lack in name or reality, but the effect was joy in one case and anger in another. This too is based on assumptions.

Therefore sages harmonize right and wrong, leaving them to the balance of nature. This is called double efficiency.

The knowledge of ancient people reached somewhere. Where did it reach? Some thought the ultimate is where nothing has ever existed. This is all—nothing can be added. Next they thought there is something, but without any boundaries. Next they thought there are boundaries, but without right and wrong.

The appearance of right and wrong was the reason the Way has been missing. The reason the Way is missing is the reason emotional attachment forms. But is there actually any presence or absence?

A harpist can play because of the presence and absence of the notes; without presence or absence, the harpist cannot play.

There were three maestros, a harpist, a tuner, and a philosopher, whose knowledge was virtually consummate. Each of them was successful, so they are known to posterity. Only their devotion made them different from others.

Because of their devotion, they wanted to teach. But they tried to explain what they didn't understand, and wound up in the obscurity of sophistry. And because the thread of their culture ended with their children, they died without accomplishment.

If this can be called success, then even I am also successful. If this cannot be called success, then neither I nor anyone has any success.

Therefore the aim of sages is for diffused brilliance: they do not employ it for affirmation, but entrust it to the constant. This is called using clarity.

○

Now there is a saying about this, but I don't know if it's in the same category or not. If being in the same category and not being in the same category are construed as being in the same category with each other, then there is no difference. In any case, let me try to say it.

There is a beginning, there is never beginning to have a beginning, there is never beginning to never begin to have a beginning. There is existence, there is nonexistence. There is never beginning the existence of nonexistence, there is never beginning never beginning the existence of nonexistence. Suddenly there are existence and nonexistence, but we don't know if existence or nonexistence actually exist or not.

Now I have said something, but I don't know if what I have said actually says anything or not.

○

Nothing in the world is bigger than a hair tip; a huge mountain is small.

No one lives longer than one who dies in childhood; a man who lives eight hundred years is young. Heaven and earth are born with us; all beings are one with us.

If all is one, can anything be said? Once it has been said that all is one, can nothing be said? Unity and speech make two; two plus one make three. What follows cannot be grasped even by skilled calculators, much less by ordinary people.

Therefore when you go from nonbeing to being, you thereby come to a third point. How about when you go from being to being! It is simply for this reason that there is no getting anywhere.

○

The Way has never had boundaries; language has never been constant. Borders exist because of affirmations.

Let me tell you about those borders: there is left, and there is right; there is principle, and there is justice; there is distinction, and there is discrimination; there is competition, and there is conflict. These are called eight qualities.

Outside the universe, sages see without discussion. Inside the universe, sages discuss without deliberation. When it comes to the passing times and generations and the records of kings of yore, sages deliberate without debating.

Therefore there is that which distinction does not distinguish, there is that which explanation does not explain. What is it? Sages take it to heart, average people try to explain it to each other. That is why it is said that there is something not seen by explanation.

The Great Way is not called anything: great discernment is unspoken; great humaneness is unsentimental; great honesty is not complacent; great bravery is not vicious.

When a way is illustrious, it does not guide; when humanitarianism is fixated, it is not constructive; when honesty is puritanical, it is not trusted; when bravery is vicious, it does not succeed. These five things are like looking for squareness in something round.

So we know that to stop at what we don't know is as far as we can go. Who knows the unspoken explanation, the unexpressed Way? Among those who do know, this is called the celestial storehouse: we can pour into it without filling it, we can draw from it without exhausting it; and yet we don't know where it comes from. This is called hidden illumination.

○

In ancient times King Yao told his future successor Shun that he was going to attack three nations but was not at ease in the position of a ruler. He asked Shun why. Shun replied, "The rulers of those nations are still living in the wild state. Why aren't you at ease? In ancient times ten suns appeared, illumining all things; is virtue not superior to a sun?"

○

Nieh Ch'ueh asked Wang Ni, "Do you know what beings alike affirm?"

Wang Ni replied, "How would I know this?"

Nieh Ch'ueh asked, "Do you know what I don't know?"

Wang Ni replied, "How would I know this?"

Nieh Ch'ueh asked, "Then has no one any knowledge?"

Wang Ni replied, "How would I know this? Even so, I have tried to say it. How do we know that what we call knowledge is not ignorance? How do we know that what we call not knowing is not knowledge?

"Now let me ask you something. When people sleep on damp ground, they get sacroiliac problems and even become partially paralyzed and die; is that true of a mud loach? If people perched in trees, they would be petrified; is that true of monkeys? Humans, loaches, monkeys—who knows the right place?

"Monkeys mate with other monkeys, deer mate with other deer, fish sport with fish. Certain women have been considered beautiful by all men, but fish dove into the depths on seeing them, birds flew off on seeing them, deer bolted on seeing them. Humans, fish, birds, deer—who knows what form in the world is right?

"From my point of view, the beginnings of humanity and justice, the roads of gain and loss, are mixed up—how can I know their distinctions?"

Nieh Ch'ueh said, "If you don't know what is gain or loss, then does that mean complete people do not know gain or loss?"

Wang Ni replied, "Complete people are spiritual: a huge conflagration cannot heat them, freezing cold cannot chill them, lightning storms and gale-force winds cannot upset them. If you can be like that, you can ride on the energy of the clouds, mount the sun and moon, and travel beyond the four oceans. Even death and life do not change you, much less the edges of gain and loss."

○

Master Chi-ch'iao asked Master Ch'ang-wu, "I have heard from you that sages do not engage in business; they do not strive for gain or try to avoid loss. They do not want to seek and do not get involved in any way. They make a statement by not saying anything, and they say nothing when they make a statement. Thus they roam outside the dust and dirt.

"Confucius thinks this is just a fantastic tale, but I consider it practical application of the sublime Way. What do you make of it?"

Master Ch'ang-wu said, "Even the Yellow Emperor [a legendary sage] was confused about this—so how could the likes of Confucius be able to know about it?

"And you too are jumping to conclusions: seeing an egg, you are expecting to have a rooster crowing already; seeing a bullet, you expect to have game cooking already. Let me try to give you an imaginative description, so you can listen to it imaginatively; how about that?

"Sages stand alongside the sun and moon, hold time and space in their arms. Being in a state of unity, they let confusion and obscurity be, and honor those of humble station. Whereas most people are frenetically busy, sages are innocent, merging ten thousand years into a single unadulterated whole. All things and all beings are as they are, and thereby accumulate relative to one another.

"How can I know that wanting to live is not delusion? How can I know that aversion to death is not like a homeless waif who does not know where to return?

"When a beautiful princess was taken captive by another nation, at first she cried so hard she dampened her sleeves. Then she started living with the king, sharing his bed and eating fine food; after that she regretted having wept.

"How do I know the dead do not regret having longed for life at first? Those who dream they are drinking wine cry mournfully in the morning; those who dream they are crying mournfully go out sporting in the morning. When they are dreaming, they don't know they are dreaming. As they are dreaming, they even try to divine the meanings of dreams. Only after waking up do they know they were dreaming.

"What is more, there is a great awakening, after which we know this has been a grandiose dream. Yet fools think themselves to be awake. They make subjective judgments of superior and inferior so rigidly!

"Confucius and you are both dreaming. Even my saying you are dreaming is a dream too. This kind of talk is called extremely strange; great sages such as are met but once in ten thousand generations are met daily by those who know how to interpret this.

"Suppose I have a debate with you, and you beat me, I don't beat you—does that mean you are actually right and I am actually wrong? If I beat you and you don't beat me, does that mean I am actually right and you are actually wrong? Are both right, or both wrong?

"You and I cannot know, and a third party would certainly get blinded. Who would we have determine who is correct? Suppose we had someone who was the same as you decide who is correct; how could someone who is the same as you determine who is correct? Suppose we had someone who was the same as me decide who is correct; how could someone who is the same as me determine who is correct? So I, you, and a third party cannot know—would you depend on yet another?

"What does this mean? Join them at their natural boundaries. When you say 'right' and 'not right,' 'so' and 'not so,' even if 'right' is actually right, the difference between 'right' and 'not right' is as yet undefined; even if 'so' is actually so, the difference between 'so' and 'not so' is as yet undefined.

"The relations of sounds without realities are like no relation at all. Join them at their natural boundaries, and let them develop; this is the way to live out your years. Thus you forget age, forget social conventions, and thrive in infinity, therefore putting it all in the infinite."

———o———

Nonduality asked Shadow, "Before, you were active, but now you are at rest; before, you were sitting, but now you are up and about. Why don't you behave consistently?"

Shadow said, "Do I depend on anything to be as I am? Does what I depend on then also depend on something to be as it is? Do I depend on the sloughed-off skin of a snake or the empty shell of a cicada? How would I know it is so? How would I know it is not so?"

———o———

Once Chuang Chou dreamed he was a butterfly. He was happy as a butterfly, enjoying himself and going where he wanted. He did not know he was Chou. Suddenly he awoke, whereupon he was startled to find he was Chou. He didn't know whether Chou had dreamed he was a butterfly, or if a butterfly were dreaming it was Chou. But as Chou and the butterfly, there must be a distinction. This is called the transformation of beings.

3

Mastery of Nurturing Life

Our lives are finite, but knowledge is infinite. To follow the infinite by means of the finite is perilous; thus those who still invent knowledge will only perish.

If you do not approach fame for doing good, do not get near punishment by doing ill, and focus on the center as the norm, it is possible thereby to preserve your body, fulfill your life, support your relatives, and live out your years.

———— o ————

Once a butcher was cutting up an ox for a king. As he felt with his hand, leaned in with his shoulder, stepped in and bent a knee to it, the carcass fell apart with a peculiar sound as he played his cleaver.

The king, expressing admiration, said to the butcher, "Good! It seems that this is the consummation of technique."

The butcher put down his cleaver and replied, "What I like is the Way, which is more advanced than technique. But I will present something of technique.

"When I first began to cut up oxen, all I saw was an ox. Even after three years I had still not seen a whole ox. Now I meet it with spirit rather than look at it with my eyes.

"When sensory knowledge stops, then the spirit is ready to act. Going by the natural pattern, I separate the joints, following the main apertures, according to the nature of its formation. I have never even cut into a mass of gristle, much less a large bone.

"A good butcher changes cleavers every year because of damage, a mediocre butcher changes cleavers every month because of breakage. I've had this cleaver for nineteen years now, and it has cut up thousands of oxen; yet its blade is as though it had newly come from the whetstone.

"The joints have spaces in between, whereas the edge of the cleaver blade has no thickness. When that which has no thickness is put into that which has no space, there is ample room for moving the blade. This is why the edge of my cleaver is still as sharp as if it had newly come from the whetstone.

"Even so, whenever I come to a knot, I see the difficulty to doing it. I am careful to remain alert, with my gaze steady. Moving slowly, I exert a very slight force, and the knot has come apart, like earth crumbling into the ground. Then I stand there with my cleaver, looking all around and pausing over the satisfaction in this. Then I clean off the cleaver and put it away."

The king said, "Excellent! Having heard the words of a butcher, I have found the way to nurture life."

○

Someone saw a man whose foot had been chopped off. Surprised, he said, "What kind of man are you? Why has your foot been chopped off? Did Heaven do this to you, or did people do it?"

The man with one foot said, "Heaven, not people. When Heaven created me, It destined me to have one foot. There is that in people's appearances which is given. Therefore I know it is Heaven and not people."

○

A marsh pheasant walks ten steps for bit of food, a hundred steps for a drink of water. It does not seek to be raised in a cage. Even though it might grow robust in captivity, that is not good.

When Lao Tan died, Ch'in Shih went to his funeral, where he cried out three times and left. The disciples of Lao Tan said to him, "Weren't you a friend of the master?"

Ch'in Shih replied, "Yes."

They said, "Then how can you mourn him like this?"

Ch'in Shih answered, "That's the way it is. At first I thought you were his people, but now I see you're not. When I went in to mourn just now, there were elders weeping for him the way parents weep when their children die, and there were young people weeping for him the way children weep when their mothers die. The reason for the gathering of these people must involve speaking words you haven't been asked to say, and grieving without having been asked to mourn. This is evading nature, adding sentiments, and forgetting your lot. The ancients called this punishment for trying to evade Nature.

"When the master came, it was his time; and when it was time to go, he went along. If you are at peace in your time and live harmoniously, sadness and happiness cannot affect you. Ancients called this God's release of attachments."

○

When the fingers have no more kindling to put in, the fire goes on burning, unaware that it's gone.

4

The Human World

Yen Hui visited Confucius to ask him permission to go on a journey. Confucius said, "Where are you going?"

Yen Hui replied, "I'm going to Wei."

Confucius asked, "What for?"

Yen Hui answered, "I have heard that the king of Wei is young and behaves in an arbitrary manner. He exploits his country frivolously and does not see his own errors. The people are dying from this exploitation; countless numbers have perished, and the people have nowhere to go.

"I have heard you say that we should leave orderly states and go to chaotic states; there are many sick patients at a physician's door. I want to use what I have learned to think of a way for that state to be healed."

Confucius said, "Ha! If you go anywhere near there, you'll just get punished. The Way does not like adulteration. If there is adulteration, there is complication; and if there is complication, there is unease. If there is unease, there is worry, worry that cannot help.

"People of attainment in ancient times first established it in themselves, and after that established it in others. As long as what you have established in yourself has not been stabilized, what leisure time do you have to deal with the actions of a violent man?

"And do you know, moreover, why virtue is swept away and science is made up? Virtue gets swept off by fame, and science is produced by contention.

"What fame is, as a matter of fact, is the screeching of friction. What science is, as a matter of fact, is a tool of contention. Both are instruments of ill omen and are not the way to fulfill a life's work.

"Now you are rich in virtues and solidly trustworthy, but you do not yet have perfect understanding of people's moods. You do not compete for fame, but you do not yet have perfect understanding of people's hearts.

"Under these conditions, if you insist on giving speeches about humanity, justice, and order to a violent man, this would be positing the goodness of those virtues on the evils of the man. That is what is called stabbing someone, and those who stab others will inevitably be stabbed by others. You are in danger of getting stabbed.

"Furthermore, if the king did like the wise and despise the unworthy, what need would he have of you for anything different? If you go without being invited, the king will surely take advantage of his position over people to try to beat you in a battle of wits.

"Your eyes will be dazzled by him, your face will change at this; your talk will be confused by him, your attitude will show it; and your mind will be converted to his point of view.

"This is trying to put out a blaze by means of fire, trying to stop a flood by means of water. This is called increasing what is already too much.

"If you go along in the beginning, there is no end to it. Insofar as you are not trusted, even if you speak with good intentions, you will surely die at the hands of that violent man.

"In ancient times, the tyrant Chieh killed Kuan Lung-feng, and the tyrant Chou killed the prince Pi Kan. Both Kuan Lung-feng and Pi Kan had cultivated themselves and looked after the welfare of others' subjects. This offended their superiors, and so their rulers destroyed them because of their cultivation. They were people who liked having a good reputation.

"In antiquity King Yao attacked two states, and King Yü attacked another. Those states became wastelands, and their leaders were executed. They had used their military forces unceasingly and continually sought material gain.

"These were all people who sought name or gain. Have you alone not heard of them? Name and gain are things that even sages cannot override, let alone someone like you.

"Nevertheless, you must have a reason. You might as well go ahead and tell me about it."

Yen Hui asked, "How about if I am upright and unassuming, diligent and wholehearted?"

Confucius said, "How? How would that do? The king is full of aggressive energy, and extremely high-strung. He is emotionally unstable, and no one ever contradicts him. He suppresses the feelings of others as he seeks to indulge in his own wishes.

"This is called failure to accomplish even the virtues that build up gradually in day-to-day living; great virtue is out of the question. He will stick to his ways and not change for the better. If you harmonize outwardly and fail to criticize inwardly, how could that do any good?"

Yen Hui asked, "Then what if I am inwardly honest, outwardly tactful, and make judgments with reference to the ancients?

"Those who are inwardly honest are companions of Nature. Those who are companions of Nature know that emperors and themselves are all children of Nature. So why would they care about others' approval or disapproval of what they say? Such people are called innocents; this is what it means to be companions of Nature.

"Those who are outwardly tactful are companions of people. The various courtesies and manners of people in the service of others are things that everyone does; how dare I not do them? If you do as others do, then no one will criticize you; this is called being a companion of people.

"Those who make judgments with reference to the ancients are companions of the ancients. Although what they say is instructive, there is a critical core to it; this is attributed to the ancients, not to an individual, so even if they are honest they are not resented. This is called being a companion of the ancients.

"If I were like this, would that do?"

Confucius replied, "How? How would that do? Too many governing principles, and unsure besides. Although this way of yours is not progressive, still it will keep you from being charged with a crime; but that's all. How can it be enough to effect reform? You are still following your own inclinations."

Yen Hui said, "I have nothing more to offer. May I ask you for a suitable method?"

Confucius replied, "Fast. I will tell you how. If you try to do it deliberately, how can it be easy? Those who consider it easy are not approved under the clear sky."

Yen Hui said, "My family is poor, and we go for months on end without drinking wine or eating meat. Can this be considered fasting?"

Confucius answered, "That is the kind of fasting one does for religious rituals; it is not mental fasting."

Yen Hui inquired, "May I ask about mental fasting?"

Confucius replied, "You unify your will: hear with the mind instead of the ears; hear with the energy instead of the mind. Hearing stops at the ears, the mind stops at contact, but energy is that which is empty and responsive to others. The Way gathers in emptiness; emptiness is mental fasting."

Yen Hui said, "The reason I haven't been able to master this is that I consider myself really me. If I could master this, 'I' would not exist. Could that be called emptiness?"

Confucius answered, "That's all there is to it. I tell you, you can go into that corral without being moved by repute. If you are heard, then speak; if not, then stop. Let there be no dogma, no drastic measures; remain consistent and abide by necessity. Then you'll be close.

"It is easy to obliterate tracks, hard not to walk on the ground. It is easy to use falsehood in working for people; it is hard to use falsehood in working for Nature.

"I have heard of flying with wings; I have never heard of flying without wings. I have heard of knowing with knowledge; I have never heard of knowing without knowledge.

"For those who gaze into space, the empty room produces white light; auspicious signs hover in stillness. But if one does not stay here, that is called galloping even while sitting.

"If you have your ears and eyes penetrate inwardly, and are detached from conceptual knowledge, then even if ghosts and spirits come after you they will stop; how much the more will people!

"This is the evolution of myriad beings. This is what [the sage kings] Yü and Shun were rooted on, what [prehistoric cultural leaders] Fu Hsi and Chu Chi practiced all their lives. How much greater is the need of those who have already lost it!"

○

When Tzu-kao, duke of She, was going to serve as an ambassador to the state of Ch'i, he asked Confucius about it, saying, "The king has sent me on a mission; this is very serious. Ch'i treats ambassadors very respectfully, but won't hurry. Even their ordinary men cannot be moved; how much less their lords! I am very concerned about this.

"You once told me that whether matters are small or great, few do not say they are glad of success. If an undertaking is unsuccessful, there is inevitably some trouble with people; even if an undertaking is successful, there is inevitably some trouble with the balance of energy. Only those who are endowed with virtue can be free from trouble whether or not they have succeeded in accomplishing something.

"My fare is coarse, not fine; no one would seek relief from the heat in my kitchen. But now I have received the orders for this mission in the morning, and am drinking ice water at night. Could I have become fevered within? Before anything has even happened, I am already having trouble with my balance of energy. And if this affair is unsuccessful, I will have trouble with people. That's both!

"I am not fit for public service. Is there anything you can tell me?"

Confucius responded, "There are two great precepts in the world. One is decree, the other is duty. For children to love their parents is decree; it cannot be removed from the heart. For administrators to serve their governments is duty; there is government anywhere you go, so there is no place to escape between heaven and earth. These are called the major precepts.

"Therefore the perfection of filial devotion is to take care of your parents in such a way that they are at peace wherever they are. The fulfillment of loyalty is to serve the government in such a way that all matters are peacefully settled, no matter what they are.

"The perfection of virtue is to take care of your own mind in such a way that emotions cannot affect you when you already know nothing can be done, and are at peace with what is, with the decree of fate.

"As a public servant, you definitely have no choice in the matter. Carry out the task truthfully, and forget about yourself. What leisure time have you to hope for survival and worry about dying? You should go.

"And let me add something I've heard. In relations with those nearby, it is necessary to win each other over by trustworthiness. In relations with those afar, it is necessary to be truthful to them in words.

"Words need someone to transmit them. The hardest thing in the world is to transmit communications between two parties who are both pleased or two parties who are both angry. If both are pleased, there will be an overflow of fine words; if both are angry, there will be an overflow of ugly words. Whatever is excessive is artificial, and the artificiality makes it hard to believe. When the message is dubious, the messenger is in danger.

"Therefore a standard saying has it, 'Communicate the enduring reality, not the excessive verbiage, and you will be close to safety.'

"Furthermore, those who use cleverness to content may start out positive, but always end up negative; in extreme cases there is a lot of bizarre cunning. Those who drink wine socially may start out mannerly but always wind up slovenly; in extreme cases there is a lot of weird play. Ordinary affairs are also like this; they may start out genuine, but always turn out base. The initiating actions may be simple, but as you near the end the matter is always magnified.

"Words are airwaves; those who act on them have lost reality. The fact is that it is easy to be moved by airwaves, and when reality is lost it is easy to be vulnerable. Therefore anger is set up for no reason but the biased rhetoric of cunning talk.

"A dying animal does not choose the tone of its death rattle; its breathing is choked. All become disturbed in mind at this. If people are pressed too hard, they will inevitably respond in a bad mood, even without realizing it. If they don't realize what is going on, who knows when it will end?

"Therefore a standard saying has it, 'Let there be no changing directives, let there be no urging completion.'

"To go beyond measure is excess: changing directives and urging completion are dangerous things. A fine accomplishment takes a long time; when something is done wrongly, it's too late to change. Can we not be careful?

"Now then, if you ride on things so as to let your mind go free, and trust in necessity so as to develop balance, that is best.

"What would you make up for a report? It is best just to deliver your charge. This is what is hard."

○

When Yen Ho was going to become the guardian of the crown prince of Lord Ling of Wei, he asked Chu Po-yü, "There is someone here whose character is naturally malevolent. If I take no measures with him, then I endanger my country. If I do take measures with him, I endanger myself. He knows enough to know when people make mistakes, but not enough to know why they make mistakes. What can I do about someone like that?"

Po-yü said, "Good question! Be careful, be prudent, be correct yourself! As far as appearances are concerned, nothing compares to conformity. As far as attitude is concerned, nothing compares to harmony. Nevertheless, there are problems with both of these.

"When you conform, you don't want to be absorbed, and when you harmonize you don't want to stand out. If by appearing to conform you become absorbed, you will be upset, destroyed, ruined, downtrodden. If you stand out for your interest in cooperation, that will turn into a reputation that will be harmful to you.

"If for now he is childish, you too be childish with him. If for now he is unruly, you too be unruly with him. If for now he is unrestrained, you too be unrestrained with him. Eventually lead him into impeccability.

"Don't you know how the mantis thrusts its arms against an oncoming vehicle, not knowing it isn't up to the task? This is how it is with those who consider their talents fine. Be careful, be prudent! If you build up pride in your excellence and thereby run afoul of that person, this is dangerous.

"Don't you know that tiger keepers don't dare to feed them live animals, because of the fury of the tigers killing the prey? And they will not give them whole carcasses either, for the fury of the tigers rending them. By gauging the timing of their hunger and satiety, they guide their furious tempers.

"Tigers are a different species than humans, but they are nice to their keepers, as long as their keepers deal with them according to their nature. Those whom tigers kill are those who deal with them in a manner contrary to their nature.

"Suppose a man loves his horse so much that he provides it with a toilet and urinal. And suppose flies gather on the horse, as tends to happen. If the man tries to brush the flies away at the wrong time, the horse will bolt, breaking its neck and breastbone. The intention has an aim, but love suffers a loss. Can one not be careful?"

○

A craftsman going to the state of Ch'i came to a certain mountain and saw an enormous tree at a shrine there. That tree was so big that thousands of oxen could stand in its shade. Its trunk was so thick that it would take a hundred people to reach around it. It was so high it faced on the mountains; the first branches were seven thousand feet up. Dozens of those branches were themselves massive enough to be made into boats.

Although there were so many tourists looking at the great tree that they could have filled a city, the craftsman paid it no mind and went on his way without stopping.

One of the craftsman's apprentices gazed at the tree for a long while, then ran to catch up with the master. The apprentice said, "Since the day I took up my ax to follow you, I have never seen such fine raw material as this. Yet you won't even look at it, but just pass on by. Why?"

The master craftsman said, "Stop! Don't say it! That is an unemployable tree. A boat made from it would sink; a coffin made from it would rot. An implement made from it would quickly fall apart. If used for a door, it would dribble sap. If used for pillars, it would be eaten by insects. This is a tree that does not produce lumber; none of it can be used. That is why it has been able to get so old."

After the craftsman got home, the spirit of the shrine of the great tree appeared to him in a dream and said, "With what do you compare me? Do you compare me to a domesticated tree? Those who belong to the category of fruit-bearing trees, bushes, and vines are stripped and denuded when their fruits ripen, big branches broken and small branches torn off. These are the ones who make their lives miserable by their abilities. Because of this, they do not live out their natural years, but die untimely deaths on the way. They are the ones who get themselves struck down by the conventional world.

"Everyone is like this, so I have long sought to be unexploitable. Now I have finally attained it, after having been near to death, and it is of great use to me. If I were to be usable, could I have got this big?

"Furthermore, you and I are both creatures; how can we treat each other objectively? You are a useless man near to death; how can you know an unemployable tree?"

When he woke up, the craftsman analyzed his dream. An apprentice said, "If he was eager to be useless, why did he become a sacred tree?"

The master craftsman said, "Be silent, don't say that. He is just lodging there. He thinks that those who don't know him would vilify him. Even if he hadn't become a shrine, would he be cut down? And what he maintains is different from the crowd, so isn't it off the mark to praise him in terms of conventional principles?"

○

Once on a journey Tzu-ch'i saw a huge tree with strange knots, big enough to shelter a thousand chariots in its shade. Tzu-ch'i said, "What kind of tree is this? It must have unusual potential."

Looking up at its branches, he saw they were too crooked to be used as beams. Looking down at its roots, he saw it was not solid enough to be used for coffins. When he tasted the leaves, his mouth became inflamed; and they had a smell that would madden a person for days.

Tzu-ch'i said, "This is in fact a useless tree. That's how it got to be this big."

Yes, this is why sages cannot be exploited.

○

There is a place in the state of Sung where the conditions are right for several varieties of trees known for their straight trunks. Those of a certain size are cut by people looking to make stakes to tie monkeys. Larger ones are cut by people looking for imposing house frames. Yet larger ones are cut by people looking for material to make coffins for nobles and rich merchants. Therefore those trees never fulfill their natural age, but succumb to the ax along the way. This is the trouble with usefulness.

Therefore an ox with a white forehead, a pig with a high snout, or a person with piles are not supposed to be used in expiatory rites. All shamans know this, and consider them inauspicious. This is what spiritual people consider very auspicious.

Once there was a hunchback whose chin was buried in his navel, his shoulders higher than the top of his head. His top-knot pointed to the sky, his vital organs were on top, his thighs were at his sides. He earned enough to feed himself by doing sewing and laundry; he earned enough to feed ten people by refining grain.

Whenever the government drafted men for military action, the hunchback went about his business without fear; whenever the government drafted men for corvée labor, the hunchback was not assigned any work because of his "handicap." When the government provided for the ailing, he received bushels of grain and bundles of kindling.

Those who are physically different can take care of themselves and live out their natural years thereby. How much the more so can those who are morally different!

○

When Confucius journeyed to Ch'u, a madman of Ch'u went to him and said, "O phoenix, O phoenix, what can be done about the deterioration of virtue? Future ages cannot be counted on, past ages cannot be pursued. When the world has the Way, sages succeed in it; when the world lacks the Way, sages just live in it.

"At the present time, all one can do is escape punishment. Fortune is lighter than a feather, yet no one knows how to carry it. Calamity is heavier than the earth, yet no one knows how to avoid it.

"Stop confronting people with virtue; it is dangerous to leave a trail as you go. Hide your light, and no one will interfere with your activity. Be empty and tactful, and no one will trip you up.

"The trees in the mountains bring on their own exploitation; a candle burns itself out. Cinnamon is cut because it can be eaten; lacquer trees are split because they can be used. Everyone knows the use of the useful, but no one knows the use of the useless."

5

Tallying with Fulfillment of Virtue

In the state of Lu there was a man named Wang T'ai who had had one of his feet chopped off [by the government]. He had as many followers as Confucius.

Ch'ang Chi asked Confucius, "Wang T'ai is a man who has had a foot chopped off, yet his followers are so numerous that you and he have divided the state of Lu in half. He does not give instructions or hold discussions, yet people go to him empty and come back fulfilled. Does he indeed have an unspoken teaching, a formless way of mental development? Who is this man?"

Confucius said, "He is a sage. The only reason I haven't gone to him is simply that I have been dilatory. Even I would consider him a teacher; how much the more would those who are not a match for me! I would invite the whole continent to follow him, not just the state of Lu."

Ch'ang Chi said, "He is one of those who has had a foot chopped off, and yet is greater than you, the educator Confucius? He must be very far from ordinary. If it is as you say, what can you tell me about how he has mastered mind?"

Confucius said, "Death and life are indeed important, yet cannot get him to change. Even if heaven and earth overturn and fall, that cannot deal him any loss. He is clear about where there is nothing temporal, and does not shift along with things. He directs the evolution of things, and is keeper of their source."

Ch'ang Chi said, "What does that mean?"

Confucius said, "When you look in terms of their difference, even the liver and gall bladder are separate. When you look in terms of their sameness, all things are one.

"Assuming that is so, he does not concern himself with what ear and eye prefer, and lets his mind wander in the peaceful harmony of the virtue of equality. He looks at the unity of things, and does not see any loss. He sees the loss of his foot as like dropping a quantity of earth."

Ch'ang Chi said, "He does this for himself by means of his knowledge. He grasps his mind by means of his mind. He has attained the normal mind; why do people consider him outstanding?"

Confucius said, "People cannot use flowing water for a mirror; they use still water for a mirror. Only the still can still the masses so they become still. Of all that receives life from the earth, the pine and cedar stand out for being green through winter and summer. Of all who received life from heaven, only [the sage king] Shun alone was upright, and luckily was able to live right and thereby straighten out the lives of others.

"The effect of preserving the beginning is real fearlessness. A single warrior may be so brave as to plunge into nine armies, so even someone who disciplines himself in search of fame can be like this; how much the more someone who directs heaven and earth and governs myriad things, who just regards the body as a lodging, who considers the ears and eyes as images, who unifies his knowledge, and whose mind never dies? He will choose the day he ascends to the infinite. That is why people follow him; why would he be concerned with anyone or anything?"

Shen-t'u Chia was a man who had had a foot chopped off. He and Tzu-ch'an of Cheng were both students of Nobody, the Old Obscure One.

Tzu-ch'an said to Shen-t'u Chia, "When I go out first, you stay; when you go out first, I'll stay."

The next day they were again sitting together in the same room, and Tzu-ch'an said to Shen-t'u Chia, "When I go out first, you stay; when you go out first, I'll stay. I'm going out now, so would you stay? When you see those who hold the reins of government, you don't get out of the way. Are you equal to those who hold the reins of government?"

Shen-t'u Chia said, "Certainly there are people in our teacher's school who hold the reins of government, but do they have to be like this? You are so delighted by the fact that you yourself are holding the reins of government that you have fallen behind other people. I have heard it said that 'when a mirror is clear, that means dust has not settled on it; when dust settles on it, it becomes unclear. If you associate with good and wise people for a long time, you may become impeccable.' Now the source of your greatest gains is our teacher, and yet you talk like this; haven't you gone too far?"

Tzu-ch'an said, "You are in this condition, yet you want to argue over good planning with a wise king. Your virtue isn't even enough to look after yourself."

Shen-t'u Chia said, "Many are those who confess their own misdeeds and claim they don't deserve to die. Few are those who don't confess their misdeeds but claim they don't deserve to live. To know when nothing can be done and to be at peace with that, as if it were destiny, is something of which only those with virtue are capable. When you are wandering around in the range of a master archer, those in the middle are on ground zero; if you still don't get hit in spite of that, it is by fate.

"Many people have laughed at me for not having my feet intact, because they had both of them. I would get irritated and angry, but when I went to our teacher's place I would forget about it and be restored, not knowing the teaching was washing me with goodness. I have been with the teacher for nineteen years, and he has never noticed that I was one of those who have had a foot chopped off.

"Now you and I are roaming in a realm that is in the interior of the physical body, and yet you are making demands on me in terms of the exterior of the physical body. Isn't that a mistake?"

Startled and embarrassed, Tzu-ch'an changed his attitude and said, "Say no more."

○

In the state of Lu a certain man whose foot had been chopped off repeatedly came to see Confucius.

Confucius said to him, "You got into trouble like this because you were not prudent before. What can you do about it from now on?"

The footless one replied, "I just didn't know what I should do and used my body carelessly; that is how I lost my foot. The reason I am coming here now is that I still have something more valuable than a foot, and therefore I'm trying to keep it intact.

"Heaven covers all, earth bears all. I considered you like heaven and earth; how could I have known you'd still be like this?"

Confucius said, "I am being narrow-minded. Why don't you come in and talk about what you've learned?"

But the footless one left.

Confucius said to his disciple, "You should work diligently on this. That was a man who had his foot chopped off, yet still strives to learn in order to compensate for the faults in his previous actions. How much more will someone who would keep virtue intact!"

The footless one said to Lao Tan, "Confucius has not reached human completeness; otherwise why could he come to study from you so attentively? He even seeks fame, which is a deceptive illusion, not knowing that completed people consider it a fetter to them."

Lao Tan said, "Why not get him to consider death and life one thread, get him to consider approval and disapproval one continuity, thus freeing him from his fetters?"

The footless one said, "Heaven is punishing him; how can he be released?"

○

Lord Ai of Lu asked Confucius, "In Wei there is a hideous man named Ai T'ai-t'o. When men are with him, they cannot bear to leave; when women see him, they ask their parents to give them to him, saying they would rather be his concubine than the principal wife of another man. This has happened dozens of times, and still goes on.

"I have never heard of him initiating anything; he always just harmonizes with others. He has no position of authority whereby he could save people from dying, he has no accumulation of wealth whereby he could fill people's bellies. And he startles everyone with his ugliness.

"He harmonizes but does not initiate, his knowledge does not go beyond the four quarters, but men and women gather in his presence. He must be different from other people in some way.

"I summoned him to court to have a look at him, and found that he is indeed amazingly ugly. Before he had stayed with me for even a month, I got some idea of his character. Before a year was out, I came to trust him. As the state had no prime minister at the time, I handed the affairs of state over to him.

"He responded only after an inward struggle, and gave a vague refusal. I was ashamed, and finally handed the state over to him. Before long he left me and went away. I feel sad about this, as though I've lost something. It is as if there were no one with whom to enjoy the country. Who is that man?"

Confucius said, "Once on a journey I saw some piglets suckling from a dead sow. After a while, they all suddenly left her and ran away, because she paid no attention to them. It is simply that you are not in the same category as he. Those who love their mothers do not love their bodies, they love what animates their bodies.

"When people die in wars, they are buried without ceremonial adornments; people whose feet have been chopped off do not care about shoes. In either case there is no basis.

"The mistresses of an emperor do not cut their nails or pierce their ears. Men who are going to marry stop going out and do not work for a time. People are willing to do these things even for the sake of keeping their bodies intact; how about someone who would keep virtue intact?

"This Ai T'ai-t'o is trusted without having said anything; he is liked without having done anything. He causes people to give him their own countries and to fear only that he will not accept. He must be one whose resources are intact and whose virtue does not show in a formal way."

Lord Ai asked, "What does it mean to have one's resources intact?"

Confucius said, "Death and life, survival and extinction, failure and success, poverty and riches, worthiness and unworthiness, blame and praise, hunger and thirst, cold and heat— the changes of these things are the action of destiny. They shift back and forth day and night in our presence, but knowledge cannot encompass their beginning. Therefore they are not enough to disturb harmony and cannot get into the abode of the spirit. That makes one peaceful and contented, getting through without losing joy. To make this continuous day and night, and be as springtime to living beings, this is connecting with and giving life to the seasons in the mind. This is called having resources intact."

"What does it mean to say that virtues do not show in a formal way?"

"Still water is the most level thing in the world; it can be used as a model, inwardly maintaining evenness while not flowing outwardly. Virtue is the cultivation of completeness and harmony. People cannot leave one whose virtue does not show formally."

Another day, Lord Ai said to Master Min [who was one of the pupils of Confucius], "At first I ruled the land holding to the order of the people and worrying that they may die. I thought this was as far as one could go, but now that I have heard the words of a complete man, I am afraid I have no real attainment, that I am using my body carelessly and will lose the state. The relationship between Confucius and me is not that of ruler and subject; we are just moral companions."

○

Once there was a hunchback with clubbed feet, a deformed body, and no lips. He lectured to a certain lord, who like him so much that he came to look upon people who were physically intact as having skinny necks. Another hunchback, with a huge goiter, lectured to a lord, and the lord liked him so much that he came to see healthy people as having skinny necks. Thus when there is excellence of character, physical appearance is forgotten. When people do not forget what to forget, but forget what not to forget, that is really forgetting.

○

So sages have a place to roam. Knowledge is a by-product; contracts are glue; virtues are for making connections; crafts are for business. Sages do not scheme, so why do they need knowledge? They do not split apart, so why do they need glue? They have no loss, so why do they need virtues? They do not commercialize, so why do they need business? These four things are natural endowments, and natural endowments are the food of nature. Once you receive food from nature, what need have you of people?

Have a human appearance without having human feelings. By having a human appearance, you mix in with others; by not having human feelings, you are inaccessible to judgments of right and wrong. On the one hand, you will be small enough to associate with other people, while on the other hand, you will be great enough to attain to the celestial on your own.

○

Hui-tzu asked Chuang-tzu, "Do human beings originally have no feelings?"

Chuang-tzu said, "Yes."

Hui-tzu continued, "If people have no feelings, how can they be called human?"

Chuang-tzu said, "The Way gives them their appearance, Nature gives them their form; how can they not be called human?"

Hui-tzu asked, "If they are human, how can they have no feelings?"

Chuang-tzu said, "Judgments of right and wrong are what I am calling feelings. What I call having no feelings is when people do not harm themselves inwardly by likes and dislikes, but always go by what is natural and not try to add to life."

Hui-tzu retorted, "If people do not foster life, how can they exist?"

Chuang-tzu said, "The Way gives them their appearance; Nature gives them their form. They shouldn't let likes and dislikes harm them inwardly. Now you are directing your spirit outwardly and belaboring your vitality. You lean against a tree and sing, rest on a branch and doze. Nature has chosen your form; you are just spouting sophistry."

6

The Great Teacher of the Source

Those who know what Nature does and know what humanity does have arrived. Those who know what Nature does live naturally. Those who know what humanity does use what their knowledge knows to nurture what their knowledge does not know. Living out their natural years, not dying prematurely along the way, they are rich in knowledge, but they still have a problem.

That is the fact that knowledge depends on something to be accurate, and what it depends on is itself uncertain. How do we know that what we call divine is not human, and what we call human is not divine?

Well, there have to be real people before there is real knowledge. What do I mean by real people?

Real people of ancient times did not oppose minorities, did not lionize successes, and did not scheme things up. Being thus, they were not sorry when they were wrong, and they were not smug when they were right.

So they were not frightened in high places, did not get wet in water, were not scorched by fire. This is how knowledge can ascend to the Way.

Real people of ancient times slept without dreams and awoke without worries. Their food was not sweet, their breathing was very deep.

Real people breathe from their heels; ordinary people breathe from their throats.

Those who are stifled speak from their throats as if choking. Those whose cravings and desires are deep-seated are shallow in their celestial potential.

Real people of ancient times did not know to like life and hate death. They came to life without rejoicing and went to death without resisting; they simply came unencumbered and went unencumbered. They did not forget their beginnings or look for their end. They accepted their lot gladly, then returned it without minding.

This is called not diminishing the Way by the mind, not trying to help the divine by means of the human. Such are called real people.

Those who are thus have a focused mind, a quiet countenance, and a relaxed brow. They are cool as autumn, warm as spring; their emotions correspond to the four seasons. They have expedients for dealing with people, and none know their limit.

Therefore when sages deploy military forces, they may suffer the nation to perish but will not lose the hearts of the people. They bestow benefits on ten thousand generations, not for love of individual people.

Therefore those who are eager to communicate with people are not sages. Those who have familiars are not humane. Those who go ahead of time are not wise. Those who do not comprehend what is beneficial and what is harmful are not leaders. Those who act for reputation and lose themselves are not gentlemen. Those who are devoted but not genuine are not useful people.

As for the likes of famous men of old who killed themselves in political protest, they worked at others' work and adapted to others' convenience; they did not adapt to what was best for themselves.

Real people in ancient times were just and dutiful in their behavior, without being partisan. They seemed to be lacking, but did not accept anything. They were used to being alone, but were not rigid about it. They expounded their openness, and did not adorn. They were so mellow they seemed to be joyful. They acted when there was no choice. They were calm and collected to such a depth as to enhance their health, and gracious to such a degree as to stabilize their virtue. They were upright, appearing to be like society, yet transcendent and impossible to constrain. They were remote, as if they liked isolation. They were so simple they forgot to speak. They made law into a body, made courtesy into wings, made knowledge into timing, made virtue into a source to follow.

Making law their body, they were lenient in execution. Making courtesy their wings, they got along in the world thereby. Making knowledge their timing, they acted only when it was necessary. Making virtue their course, as long as they had means of locomotion they arrived at the heights; and yet people really thought they were striving.

Therefore they were unified in liking and unified in disliking; they were unified in unity and unified in disunity. Their unity was companionship with Nature, their disunity was companionship with humanity. When Nature and humanity do not overpower each other, this is called real humanity.

○

Death and life are destiny; the existence of consistency in the night and day is Nature. The existence of that which humans can do nothing about is the condition of things. They just regard Nature as a father, and even personally love it; how much the more should they regard that which is transcendent! People just regard established rulers as better than themselves, and even personally die for them; how much the more should they have regard for reality!

When springs dry up and fish are left on the ground, they keep each other moist with spittle; but that is not as good as forgetting each other in the rivers and lakes. And to praise the good and repudiate the evil is not as good as forgetting them both and becoming the Way itself.

The Great Mass burdens us with form, belabors us with life, relaxes us with old age, and gives us rest with death. Therefore what makes our life good is what makes our death good.

When a boat is hidden in a valley and a net is concealed in a marsh, they are considered secure; yet in the middle of the night a strong man can carry them away, unbeknownst to the unaware. There are convenient places to conceal the small and the large, yet it is still possible to make off with them. But if you hide the world in the world, there is no possibility of getting away. This is the great reality that is constant in all things.

○

If we are delighted even to be in a human form alone, insofar as the human form changes in myriad ways, without ever an end, the enjoyment therein must be incalculable. Therefore sages will roam where nothing can get away and everything is there. For them, youth is good and so is old age; for them, the beginning is good and so is the end. People even try to emulate them; how much the more that upon which all beings depend, that on which all creation relies?

The Way has reality and truth; it has no construction or form. It can be given but not taken; it can be attained but not seen. It is based on itself, rooted in itself; it has always been there, even before the existence of heaven and earth. It spiritualizes ghosts and gods, gives birth to heaven and earth. It is ahead of the absolute pole, without being high; it is beyond all limits without being deep. It was born before the universe, and yet is not ancient; it is senior to antiquity, and yet is not old.

Hsi Wei attained it, and thereby joined heaven and earth. Fu Hsi attained it, and thereby inherited the matrix of energy. The North Star got it, never to go off course. The sun and moon got it, never to come to a halt. K'an P'ei attained it, and thereby inherited the K'un-lun mountains; P'ing I attained it, and thereby roamed the great river. Chien Wu attained it, and thereby gained his place on T'ai-shan. The Yellow Emperor attained it, and thereby ascended into the clouds and sky. The god of the north attained it, and thereby came to live in the palace of darkness. The spirit of water attained it, and thereby came to stand on the north pole. The Queen Mother of the West attained it, and thereby came to sit on Mount Shao-kuang.

No one knows its beginning; no one knows its end. Grandfather P'eng attained it, and lived for hundreds of years. Fu Shuo attained it, and became the prime minister of an ancient emperor, took control of the whole country, then ascended to the firmament as one of the stars.

○

Tzu-ch'i asked Nü-yü, "You are old, and yet your face is like that of a child. Why?"

Nü-yü said, "I have heard the Way."

Tzu-ch'i asked, "Can I learn the Way?"

Nü-yü said, "How? How can you? You are not such a person.

"Now Pu-liang Yi has the talent of sages but not the Way of sages. I have the Way of sages but not the talent of sages. I wanted to teach him, so that he might actually become a sage. Even if he didn't, it is still easy to tell someone with the talent of sages about the Way of sages. But I still watched over him as I spoke to him.

"After three days he could detach from the world. Once he was detached from the world, I watched over him for another seven days, and after that he was able to detach from people and things. Once he was detached from people and things, I watched over him for another nine days, and after that he was able to detach from life. Once he was detached from life, he was able to penetrate clearly. After he had penetrated clearly, he was able to see the unique. After he had seen the unique, he could transcend time. After he had transcended time, he was able to enter into the birthless and deathless.

"What kills the living does not die; what gives birth to the living is not born. What it is brings on everything and sends off everything, breaks everything down and makes everything. Its name is peace from agitation. Peace from agitation is attained only after agitation."

Tzu-ch'i asked, "Where did you learn this?"

Nü-yü said, "I heard it from the son of Assistant Writing; the son of Assistant Writing heard it from the grandson of Thoroughly Versed; the grandson of Thoroughly Versed heard it from Seeing Clarity; Seeing Clarity heard it from Whispered Recognition; Whispered Recognition heard it from Awaiting Employment; Awaiting Employment heard it from Singing Hallelujah; Singing Hallelujah heard it from Mysterious Darkness; Mysterious Darkness heard it from High Void; High Void heard it from Uncertain Beginning."

○

Four people were talking together. Their names were Tzu Ssu, Tzu Yü, Tzu Li, and Tzu Lai. They said among themselves, "Who has nothingness for a head, life for a spine, and death for a tail? Who knows the unity of death and life, of existence and nonexistence? I would be a companion of such a person." The four looked at each other and smiled. They had no discord in mind, so they became friends.

Suddenly Tzu Yü got sick, and Tzu Ssu went to ask after him. Tzu Yü said, "How great is the creator! How cramped it has made me: I am twisted and hunchbacked, my spine is sticking out, my internal organs are on top, my chin is buried in my navel, my shoulders are higher than the crown of my head, my topknot points toward the sky, and my yin and yang energies are jumbled up. My mind, however, is free from concern."

Then, limping over to a well to look at himself in the mirrorlike surface of the water, he said, "Oh, how cramped the creator has made me!"

Tzu Ssu asked, "Do you hate it?"

Tzu Yü replied, "Why should I hate it? If it should come to pass that it turns my left arm into a rooster, I will use it to find out the dawn hour; if it should turn my right arm into a bullet, I will use it to hunt game. If it turns my buttocks into wheels and my spirit into a horse, I will use them to ride and have no more need of a car.

"Furthermore, gain is a matter of timing, loss is a matter of acceptance. If you adapt to the times and live in accord, then sadness and happiness cannot get in. This is what the ancients called release from hangups. As for those who cannot release themselves, people and things bind them. Moreover, people have never been able to overcome Nature, so why should I hate it?"

Then suddenly Tzu Lai got sick. Gasping for breath, he hovered on the brink of death, his wife and children surrounding him weeping. Tzu Li went to call on him and scolded his family, telling them to clear out and not be afraid of change. Leaning against the door, he said to Tzu Lai, "How great is the creator! What is it going to do with you? Where is it going to take you? Is it going to make you into a rat's liver, or is it going to make you into an insect's arm?"

Tzu Lai said, "When parents give directions to their children, they are obeyed. The power of yin and yang over people is even greater than that of parents over children; if they bring my death near and I do not pay heed, then I am being disobedient—what fault is it of theirs?

"The Great Mass carries me with form, belabors me with life, relaxes me with old age, and puts me to rest with death. What makes my life good is also what makes my death good.

"Now if a smith were casting metal, and the metal were to leap up and declare that it wanted to be a fine sword, the smith would surely consider it an ominous piece of metal. Now when one happens to be in a human form, if one were to insist on only being a human, the creator would surely consider one an ominous person.

"Now if you consider the universe as a great forge and the creator as a great smith, what could happen that would not be all right? I go to sleep relaxed and perk up when I wake."

When Tzu Sang-hu, Meng Tzu-fan, and Tzu Ch'in-chang became friends, they said to each other, "Who can associate with others without association; who can act for the sake of others without deliberate contrivance? Who can ascend to the heavens and roam in the mists with infinite freedom, forgetting about life and never coming to an end?"

The three looked at each other and smiled; all were in accord, so they became friends.

Not long afterward, Tzu Sang-hu died. Before the funeral, Confucius heard of this and sent his disciple Tzu-keng to attend the services. When he got there, he found one of the friends weaving a screen and the other one strumming a harp; together they were singing, "O Sang-hu, O Sang-hu—you've returned to the reality, while we, alas, are still people."

Tzu-keng stepped forward and said, "May I ask about the etiquette of singing over a corpse?"

The two friends looked at each other and smiled, saying, "What does he know about etiquette?"

Tzu-keng went back and told Confucius about this, remarking, "What kind of people are they? They make no attempt to cultivate their behavior, and they stand aloof of their physical bodies. They sing over a corpse, without any change in the expression on their faces. I have no way to label them; what kind of people are they?"

Confucius replied, "They roam outside of convention, whereas I am one of those who travels within convention. Outside and inside have no connection with each other, and yet here I have sent you to that funeral—this was my stupidity. They are people who are companions of the creator and roam in the unified energy of heaven and earth.

"They consider life an excess growth and consider death to be excision of the growth. If people are like that, how can it be known which takes precedence, life or death?

"Depending on different things lodged in one body, they forget about their livers and gall bladders. They are oblivious of their ears and eyes. They repeat the cycle over and over, not knowing where it begins. They roam infinitely beyond the dust and dirt, freely sporting at the work of nondoing. How could they take the trouble to perform the rites of ordinary society to put on appearances for people?"

Tzu-keng said, "Then what convention do you rely on?"

Confucius said, "I am a man whom Heaven has slaughtered. Even so, I will share it with you."

Tzu-keng said, "May I ask about your way?"

Confucius said, "Fish take to water, people take to the Way. Those who take to water burrow in ponds and feed there. Those who take to the Way have no concerns, and their lives are stabilized. Therefore it is said, 'Fish forget about each other in rivers and lakes; people forget each other in arts of the Way.' "

Tzu-keng said, "May I ask about extraordinary people?"

Confucius replied, "Extraordinary people are different from other people; they are on a par with Nature. Therefore it is said that a small person to Nature is a leader to men, and a leader of men is a small person to Nature."

○

Yen Hui asked Confucius, "When his mother died, Meng-sun Ts'ai wept without shedding tears, his inner mind was not stricken with grief, and he went through the mourning period without sadness. Even without these three things he has become known throughout the state of Lu for how well he mourned. Is there such a thing as getting the name without having the reality? I am very suspicious of this."

Confucius said, "Mr. Meng-sun has done it all. He has gone beyond knowledge. He would have simply eliminated this, but he couldn't; yet he himself did eliminate something. Mr. Meng-sun isn't aware of the wherefore of life or the wherefore of death. He doesn't know whether to go earlier or later. It seems he goes along with evolution as a creature, thus awaiting developments unknown to him.

"Furthermore, when transformation is taking place, how can one know the unchanging? When transformation is not taking place, how can one know the aftermath of change? Are you and I the only ones who have never awakened from dreams?

"He, in contrast, may experience change in form, but it doesn't depress him psychologically; he may experience change in abode, but it doesn't deplete him emotionally. Mr. Meng-sun is particularly awakened. When people cry, he also cries; this is itself the way he adapts.

"For the time being, we consider each other as selves, that is all; how can we know what we are referring to by calling it the self? If you dream you are a bird, you soar into the sky; if you dream you are a fish, you plunge into the deep. Who knows whether the present speaker is awake or dreaming?

"When one attains comfort, there is no need to try to smile; when one shows a smile, there is no need to force it. When one manages to leave the process of change, one then enters the silent unity of Heaven."

○

When I-erh-tzu saw Hsü Yu, Hsü Yu said to him, "What has King Yao given you?"

I-erh-tzu said, "Yao told me I must practice humanity and justice, and clearly say what is right and what is wrong."

Hsü Yu said, "What have you come here for? Yao has already tattooed your face for your humanity and justice, and has cut off your nose for your judgment of right and wrong. How will you roam in freedom and view the path of evolution?"

I-erh-tzu said, "Even so, I wish to roam on the periphery of that domain."

Hsü Yu said, "No. The blind cannot relate to physical beauty; those without eyes cannot gaze on colors."

I-erh-tzu said, "When a famous beauty of old gave up her beauty, and a strong man gave up his strength, and an intellectual gave up his knowledge, in each case it was through the refinement of creation. Who knows but that the creator may remove my tattoo and restore my nose, enabling me to take advantage of completeness and follow you?"

Hsü Yu said, "Well, who knows? I will tell you the general outline.

"As for what my teacher is, my teacher harmonizes myriad beings, but does not consider that justice; its blessings extend to myriad generations, but it does not consider that humanity. It is senior to high antiquity, but doesn't consider that being old. Covering and supporting heaven and earth, it sculpts myriad forms, yet doesn't consider that skillful. This is just the realm of its sport, that's all."

○

Yen Hui said to Confucius, "I have made progress."

Confucius said, "What do you mean?"

Yen Hui said, "I have forgotten about humanity and duty."

Confucius said, "That's all right, but still not enough."

Another day, Yen Hui saw Confucius again and said, "I have made progress."

Confucius said, "What do you mean?"

Yen Hui said, "I have forgotten about ritual and music."

Confucius said, "That's all right, but still not enough."

Another day, Yen Hui saw Confucius again and said, "I have made progress."

Confucius said, "What do you mean?"

Yen Hui said, "I sit in forgetfulness."

Startled, Confucius said, "What do you mean by sitting in forgetfulness?"

Yen Hui said, "I ignore my body and dismiss my intelligence: detaching from physical form and leaving knowledge behind, I assimilate to the Universal. This I call sitting in forgetfulness."

Confucius said, "When there is sameness, there are no preferences; when there is change, there is no constant. Are you actually so wise? I would follow you."

○

Tzu Yü and Tzu Sang were friends. Once, when it had rained continuously for ten days, Tzu Yü said, "Tzu Sang is in danger of starving," and he wrapped up some food and went to feed him.

When he got to Tzu Sang's door, Tzu Yü heard him singing, or crying, as he strummed a lute, "Is it my father? Is it my mother? Is it Heaven? Is it humanity?" At times he was too weak to raise his voice, and recited his verse hurriedly.

Tzu Yü went in and said, "Why is your song like this?"

Tzu Sang said, "I have been trying to think of who has brought me to this extremity, but I cannot find out. How could my parents have wanted me to be poor? Heaven covers all impersonally, earth supports all impersonally; how could they have personally inflicted me with poverty? I have searched for who has done this, but I cannot find out; so to have come to this extremity must be a matter of fate."

7

Responsive Leadership

Teeth Missing questioned Royal Child four times; all four times Royal Child answered that he didn't know. Teeth Missing jumped for joy at this. He went to tell Willow-Clothed Philosopher.

Willow-Clothed Philosopher said, "Did you just realize this now? The ancient emperor Shun was not as good as the yet more ancient emperor T'ai. Shun still embosomed humanity to seek people and form bonds with them. And he did win people, but he never got out of repudiating people.

"When T'ai lay down, he was relaxed, and when he awoke he was content. He would consider himself a horse, and he would consider himself an ox. His knowledge was truly reliable; his virtue was very real. And yet he never entered into repudiating people."

---

o

When Bearing Self saw Crazy Chariot-Grabber, he asked him, "What did Midday Beginning tell you?"

Bearing Self said, "He told me, 'If a leader personally expresses the norm and rules people with justice, who would dare not obey and conform?'"

Crazy Chariot-Grabber said, "This is bogus virtue. It is about as feasible for governing the world as it would be to walk across an ocean, dig out a river, or have a mosquito carry a mountain on its back.

"Is the government of sages government of externals? It is simply a matter of acting only when correct, making certain of the ability to do one's work; that is all.

"Furthermore, birds fly high to avoid being hit by arrows, rats burrow deep under shrines to avoid being smoked out or dug out. Are you more ignorant than these two creatures?"

○

Heaven's Root traveled to Yin-yang, and came to the Liao River, where he happened to meet Nameless Man. He said to him, "Let me ask about working for the world."

Nameless Man said, "Go away. You are an ignoramus. What an unpleasant question!

"I would be a partner of the creator; and when I tire of that, I will ride on the bird of uncharted vastness to soar beyond the universe, roam in the realm of nothingness, and alight in the fields of infinity. So what are you doing bothering me about governing the world?"

Heaven's Root questioned him again. Nameless Man said, "Set your mind free in calmness, combine your energy with openness, harmonize with things naturally, and do not allow selfish bias therein. Then the world will be orderly."

○

Yang Tzu-chü visited Lao Tan and said, "There is someone here who is swift and strong, incisive and intelligent, and studies the Way tirelessly. Can such a person be compared with an enlightened king?"

Lao Tan said, "This is someone who is changed by knowledge and chained by skill, one who belabors his body and upsets his mind.

"Furthermore, the markings of tigers and leopards bring hunters; the quickness of monkeys and the hunting ability of dogs get them chained up. How can this be compared to enlightened kings?"

Startled, Yang Tzu-chü said, "Dare I ask about the government of enlightened kings?"

Lao-tzu said, "The achievement of enlightened kings covers the whole land, yet appears not to come from themselves. Their civilizing influence is bestowed on all beings, yet the people do not feel dependent on it. It is there, but no one mentions it, so the people may rejoice on their own. Enlightened kings stand on the unfathomable and roam in nonbeing."

O

In the country of Cheng there was a shaman named Chi Hsien. He could tell whether people were going to die or live, survive or perish, suffer misfortune or attain prosperity, live long or die young; and he could tell all this to the year, month, week, and day, as if he were a spirit. The people of Cheng all ran away when they saw him.

When Lieh-tzu met this shaman, he was fascinated, and went back to tell [his own mentor] the Master of the Pot. Lieh-tzu said to the master, "At first I thought your Way was supreme, but there is one that is yet more perfect."

The Master of the Pot said to Lieh-tzu, "What I have given you covers the appearance, but not the reality. Do you think you have attained the Way? How can a bunch of hens lay fertile eggs without a rooster? You use the Way to compete with society, and insist on being believed; that is why people can read your features. As a test, bring the shaman here and let him see me."

The next day Lieh-tzu brought the shaman to visit the Master of the Pot. After they left, the shaman said to Lieh-tzu, "Your teacher is a dead man; he cannot live. He has less than ten days. I see something strange in him; I see wet ashes there."

Weeping so much that he wet his chest, Lieh-tzu told the Master of the Pot about this.

The master said, "I showed him the sign of earth, lifeless, unmoving, unstable. Likely he saw me shut down the working of my power. Try bringing him again."

The next day Lieh-tzu took the shaman to see the master

again. When they left, the shaman said to Lieh-tzu, "It's lucky that your teacher met me! He has recovered completely, and will live. I see how he had his potential shut down."

Lieh-tzu went in and told the master about this. The Master of the Pot said, "I showed him heaven and earth; name and substance do not enter, but potential emerges from the heels. Likely he saw my positive potential. Try bringing him again."

The following day Lieh-tzu went with the shaman to see the Master of the Pot again. When they left, the shaman said to Lieh-tzu, "Your teacher is inconsistent; I cannot read his features. If he levels off, then I will read him."

Lieh-tzu went in and told the Master of the Pot about this. The master said, "I showed him the great void, which nothing can surpass. Likely he saw my state of equilibrium.

"A place where giant fish lurk is called an abyss, a place where there is still water is called an abyss, and a place where there is a current is also called an abyss. There are nine types of abyss; I have shown him three. Try bringing him again."

The next day Lieh-tzu took the shaman to see the Master of the Pot once more. Before he had even come to a standstill, the shaman lost control of himself and ran away.

The Master of the Pot said, "Go after him!"

Lieh-tzu chased the shaman, but couldn't catch him. He then went back and told the master, "He's gone, disappeared; I simply couldn't catch up with him."

The Master of the Pot said, "I showed him how it is when I don't leave my source at all. I presented him with empty passivity, so he couldn't tell who or what I was. Thus I became flexible and fluid, so he fled."

After that Lieh-tzu went home, thinking he had not even begun to learn. Not going out for three years, he did the cooking for his wife. Feeding the pigs as if he were feeding people, he became impersonal in all things. Whereas he had been cultured and refined, he returned to simplicity, stolid and independent, controlled even in the midst of bustling activity, maintaining this consistently to the end of his life.

Do not be subject to labels; do not be full of schemes; do not assume you're in charge of affairs; do not be subject to knowledge. Comprehend the infinite, and roam in the traceless.

Fulfill what you have received from Nature, without the idea of attainment; just be empty.

The attention of perfected people is like a mirror, neither sending anything off nor welcoming anything in, responding without concealment. Therefore it can transcend things and not be injured.

○

The lord of the south sea was Abrupt; the lord of the north sea was Sudden. From time to time Abrupt and Sudden got together in the territory of Primal Unity, and Primal Unity treated them very well.

Abrupt and Sudden planned to repay Primal Unity's kindness.

They said, "People all have seven openings, through which they see, hear, eat, and breathe; Primal Unity alone has none. Let us make openings in Primal Unity."

So every day they gouged out a hole. After seven days, Primal Unity died.

Notes

On the Historical Background
of Taoism, Tao Te Ching,
and Chuang-tzu

Tao is a word full of meaning. It may mean to speak, or to guide. It may mean a principle, or a system of logic. It also means a way, both in the sense of a pathway and in the sense of a method. In all of its meanings, Tao has specific and general usages. An art or a science is referred to as such and such a way, and the key to success in each particular case is called the Way of such and such an art. In its most encompassing senses, the Way means the way things are, the source of this natural order, and methods of harmonizing with the vital spirit of the Way.

In its pristine sense, the meaning of following the Tao, later called Taoism or wayfaring, included the whole spectrum of the search for knowledge. Eventually specializations branched off into a variety of schools whose interest ultimately turned into separate systems of thought and practice, each referring to its foundation of ideas as the Way. Among them, the schools of learning that retained the most comprehensive range of interest generally came to be known as Taoist to distinguish them from more narrow specialists, such as Legalists and Confucians.

The Taoist wayfarers were heirs to several sources of most ancient knowledge: shamans who knew how to alter consciousness; curers who studied the properties of plants and minerals; diviners who studied the weather, the stars, the animals, and the balance of the environment as a whole; spontaneously evolved chieftains and courts of high antiquity who laid the groundwork of civilization; court scribes and historians, whose work confronted them daily with the moral and political lessons of the ages; so-called lost people, descendants of refugee colonies founded by people of vision fleeing ancient wars, taking extended families, even whole villages, along with them; individualists, special people who were known to others but lived independently outside conventional society; and so-called sublimated or spiritualized people, who were believed to be generally unknown to ordinary humanity yet able to exert a mysterious influence under certain conditions.

Sometimes Taoist individualists, who were looked upon with awe and reverence, would participate in society, even in government, as people who could bring an extra dimension of insight to bear on the problems of the time. Sometimes families or communities of forgotten people were discovered by seekers of the Way, becoming seeds for tales of timeless immortal realms. Extraordinary stories also undoubtedly developed from encounters with other hidden people and glimpses of their unusual characters.

Thus the roots of Taoism are very old. The earliest historical Taoist text is attributed to a minister of the founder of the old Shang-Yin dynasty in the eighteenth century B.C. Taoist works are also attributed to a mentor of the father of the Chou dynasty in the twelfth century B.C. These early writings are lost, but the *Book of Change* (*I Ching*), alleged to have been composed by the founders of the Chou dynasty themselves, is also considered an ancestral Taoist text.

One of the observations of Taoist historiographers was that thinkers are more inclined to speak and act in proportion to necessity. This concept was used to explain the bursts of educational activity in times of historical crisis. Confucius and at least one of the Old Masters (Lao-tzu) of Taoism in China were more or less contemporary with Buddha in India, Zoroaster in Persia, and Pythagoras in Greece, all followers of ancient knowledge traditions working in times of political and social unrest.

In the time of Confucius and the Taoist Old Masters, the states of ancient China were competing for hegemony and clashing in sporadic civil wars that were to increase in frequency and intensity for hundreds of years. In the India of Buddha and Mahavira the great Jain, Aryan kingdoms were struggling with one another and with the indigenous Dravidian and other peoples for control of territory on the subcontinent.

The Persian Zoroaster, somewhat senior to these others, lived in the time when the Iranian Medes were breaking away from the sphere of influence of the powerful Assyrians. The city-states of Greece in the time of Pythagoras, who was not only a mathematician but primarily a philosopher, were like the Chinese states periodically at war with one another and also on the verge of war with Persia.

From Chinese Taoist descriptions, it would appear evident that society had fallen into great disorder and confusion at the time people like Confucius, Lao-tzu, Chuang-tzu, Mo-tzu, and Mencius taught and wrote about the role of culture, knowledge, and enlightenment in restoring peace and freedom in the human world.

The two essential philosophical classics of Taoism, *Tao Te Ching* and *Chuang-tzu,* were written in the later part of the Chou dynasty (1123–256 B.C.), when China was divided into competing states locked into power struggles that would consume the energies of the people for centuries to come. Both texts, responding to human emergencies, came to be regarded as political and social as well as spiritual classics.

The *Tao Te Ching* was highly regarded by strategists, legalists, and martialists as well as Taoists of all kinds; appreciation of the inner content of the *Chuang-tzu* was more limited to mystical Taoists, but its literary excellence won it general recognition as an immortal classic of allegorical fiction. Different interpretations of these texts naturally arose, some perhaps virtually as old as the second recital of either collection.

One of the major differences of opinion on the *Tao Te Ching* revolves around the issue of immortality, which was known to be of interest to some schools of Taoists, although interpreted in various different ways. Even the written wording of the text of the *Tao Te Ching* differs on this point between the versions transmitted by Legalists and those traditional among Taoists. In either case, however, the Old Master is said to prescribe methodical calmness, which is undeniably one of the major ingredients in life-prolonging recipes and exercises used by Taoists.

Scholars seem to generally believe that the author of the core inner chapters of *Chuang-tzu* repudiated the science of longevity, but the citation on which this opinion is conventionally based has been subjected to exaggeration in the specific interpretation wrought to form the foundation of this view of *Chuang-tzu*. What the classic points out is that to worry about length of life and fear death creates tension that tends to shorten life; furthermore, the life that may be prolonged by exercises is only one form or state of life, not the ultimate or universal destiny of the spirit.

The attempt to trace different elements in the roots of Taoism leads to the question of date and authorship of its texts. At the outset, it should be noted that there are many difficulties in establishing precise dates and authorship in early Chinese literature, for a number of reasons. One reason is that much of the early literature was destroyed long ago by the ravages of censorship, war, and time. Another is that date and authorship in ancient Chinese religious and philosophical literature are traditionally regarded as more important symbolically than literally.

There seems to be no question about the authorship of the inner chapters of *Chuang-tzu,* but there are various stories and theories about the authorship or compilation of the *Tao Te Ching.* The text itself suggests that it is part anthology, part recapitulation, and part commentary, drawing on ancient lore. Common legends have it that the classic was written down by Lao-tzu, whose name means the Old Master or Old Masters. This is ordinarily thought to have been Old Dan (Lao Tan), who is mentioned early on in the core chapters of *Chuang-tzu* and believed to have been an erstwhile librarian of the royal archives of the Chou dynasty and an elder contemporary of Confucius.

One of the most respected Taoist scholars of the fourth century A.D. refers to Lao-tzu as being from the time of the Shang dynasty (1766–1122 B.C.) but also includes the story that he once worked in the capacity of a librarian for the royal house of Chou, which supplanted the Shang (1122–256 B.C.). There is no doubt that the historical ancestry of the Chou dynasty Taoists dated back to Shang times, and this Taoist legend of Lao-tzu reflects the view of a scholar steeped in this tradition.

Symbolically, the combination of these two stories in effect traces the ancient knowledge represented by the Old Masters of Taoism back to Shang times, and they tell of the discovery of that knowledge "concealed" in the "library" (two meanings of the same word) of the Chou dynasty, which succeeded the Shang and inherited certain remnants of its culture.

When Taoist and Buddhist factionalists in China eventually came to compete for preeminence, one of their ploys was to back date their sages to claim greater antiquity for their own traditions. By that time, however, legendary material about ancient sages was already well established, and certain fundamental ideas could be traced back as far as the beginnings of myth and history. Exact origins of ideas and authorship of texts could not be pinned down with precision, so identifications became symbolic and classificatory rather than historical.

In the Taoist classic known as *The Masters of Huainan*, which antedates the entry of Buddhism into China, there is already a clear articulation of the idea of sages emerging into public action during times of crisis. The Buddhist view of history had a similar motif, and scholars unaware of a preexisting concord in the classics of both traditions have assumed that the idea of the reincarnation of the Taoist ancient Lao-tzu is a later Chinese borrowing from Buddhism.

In this usage, Lao-tzu the Old Master typifies the essence of Taoism, communion with the Tao, the Way. Just as in India there developed the idea of many past Buddhas before the historical Gautama Buddha, the concept of a succession of sages arose in China. Both Gautama Buddha and the author of the *Tao Te Ching* themselves refer their knowledge to earlier precedents; whether or not Taoist modes of expressing their view of history were influenced by Buddhism, Taoist legend already had the makings of this vision within it.

The idea that deterioration in the social consciousness of humanity triggered input from an extra source of knowledge existed in tales of ancient Taoist sages who became mentors and assistants of kings. Stories of personifications of the essence of the Old Master during the reigns of the leaders of antiquity traced the operation of the Tao over the ages.

The oldest known written versions of texts in the *Tao Te Ching* tradition are the two manuscripts on silk discovered in 1973 at Mawangdui. The scripts used, as well as the format of the book, suggest that these were versions of the classic as studied in the Legalist tradition. They are entitled *Te Tao Ching,* "Courses in Virtue and the Way," reversing the generally known order of the courses, and are not divided into chapters.

According to the Taoist master Liu I-ming, the Way comes to the best people before virtue, whereas virtue is needed by middling and lesser people before they can understand the Way. This would explain the order of the courses (on "virtue" and "the Way") as the text was studied in Legalist schools, since the fundamental premise of Legalism was that it is a philosophy intended for people in a degraded state.

The scripts used in the Mawangdui manuscripts would also tend to identify them as relics of the culture of the third century B.C. Ch'in dynasty, when Legalism was the dominant ideology.

Other versions of the *Tao Te Ching* are more like each other than they are like the *Te Tao Ching* transmitted by the Legalists, although there is not very much difference even between these two major categories of recension. The versions of the *Tao Te Ching* ordinarily used by Taoists and general readers derive from oral traditions written down after the Ch'in dynasty for the purpose of reviving literary and historical traditions suppressed by the militant Ch'in Legalists.

The first known arrangement of *Tao Te Ching* into the present standard format of eighty-one chapters is attributed to a mysterious Taoist known as Ho-shang Kung, or Ho-shang Chang-jen, "The Man on the River." Emperor Wen of the Han dynasty (r. 180–157 B.C.) is said to have received this version of the text directly from the Man on the River, along with a commentary by this Taoist wizard. Emperor Wen and his successor Emperor Ching (r. 157–143 B.C.) both recommended study of the classic by all officials of the central and local governments.

Many famous commentaries on *Tao Te Ching* were written by scholars of mysticism during the turbulent centuries following the end of the Han dynasty in the early third century A.D. Buddhism entered China in waves from India and Central Asia during this time, and some of the greatest Buddhist masters of the age also wrote explanations of *Tao Te Ching*. The classic was further used as a primary source for terms and concepts through which Buddhism could be explained to the Chinese.

When Buddhism came into China in the early centuries of the first millennium A.D., *Chuang-tzu* also appeared in public, emerging from the secrecy of the philosophical Taoist tradition that had gone underground in the second century B.C. when a sort of quasi-Confucianism was made the official orthodox way of thought in the Chinese empire and other philosophies were discouraged or suppressed.

The continued transmission of the teachings of Chuang Chou and his school in esoteric circles is apparent from two main sources of evidence: the early anonymous expansion of his book *Chuang-tzu* to more than four times its original length and the many citations and allusions in *Lieh-tzu, The Masters of Huainan,* and *Wen-tzu,* the great literary successors of *Chuang-tzu* in the early philosophical Taoist tradition.

After the fall of the Han dynasty that had originally imposed the quasi-Confucian orthodoxy, *Chuang-tzu* surfaced to become one of the favorite books of Chinese intellectuals, poets, and artists. In an influential movement concurrent with the influx of Buddhist ideas and arts into China, *Chuang-tzu* was studied together with the *Tao Te Ching* and the *I Ching*.

After centuries of division following the fall of the Han dynasty, China was reunited near the end of the sixth century A.D. Early in the seventh century, political control of united China was taken over by the powerful T'ang dynasty. The early emperors of T'ang China had the nobles and lords of the realm study *Tao Te Ching* and made Taoism a state religion. For a time the T'ang emperors even established official colleges of mystic studies, with *Tao Te Ching* at the head of the classics. At this time *Chuang-tzu* was formally given official recognition as a classic and ennobled with a title.

Notes to Tao Te Ching

1. *A Way Can Be a Guide*

Lines 3-4:

> Nonbeing is called the beginning of heaven and earth;
> being is called the mother of all things

This passage is also read,

> The nameless is the beginning of heaven and earth;
> the named is the mother of all things

Nonbeing, or the nameless, stands for passionless, uncontrived, formless awareness. Being, or the named, stands for discursive intellectual activity.

Lines 5-6:

> Always passionless, thereby observe the subtle;
> ever intent, thereby observe the apparent

This passage is also read,

> Eternal nonbeing is needed to observe the subtle;
> eternal being is needed to observe the manifest

These lines are one of the keys to Taoist praxis. Chen Jing-yuan, an adept of the Complete Reality school, explains,

> Both passion and intent mean focusing the mind on things. The subtle is the essential; and it also means the most extremely rarefied. The evident is an edge [of reality], like a little pathway by a major road. The word also means return [what comes back to you as a result of intentions].
> The empty selfless Tao is immutable, so it is said to have no intention; yet it becomes pregnant with myriad beings, so it is said to have passion.

To observe the subtle with constant dispassion means to keep the attention on emptiness; to observe the evident with constant intent means to sustain certain thoughts.

Constancy means real constancy, the great Way, of which dispassion and intent are adaptive functions.

Lines 7–8:

> These two come from the same source but differ in name;
> both are considered mysteries

The above mentioned two aspects of awareness, formless intuition and discursive intellect, both derive from an even profounder source. Both kinds of awareness are unfathomable mysteries, if for no other reason than that they are themselves the means by which we assess our experiences of them; and it is for the same reason that their source is by its own nature an even greater mystery.

Lines 9–10:

> The mystery of mysteries
> is the gateway of marvels

In terms of the mystic psychology of Taoism according to the Complete Reality school, this refers to the so-called "mysterious pass," the central switch post or "opening" between the rational and intuitive modes of awareness, described in the earlier passage as intentional observation of the apparent and dispassionate observation of the subtle. Taoist practice involves "opening the mysterious pass" to allow the mind to work in both modes without interference.

2.   Everyone Knows

Lines 1–4:

> When everyone knows beauty is beauty,
> this is bad.
> When everyone knows good is good,
> this is not good

According to Chen Jingyuan, this means that it is not good for people to take their own ideas for granted, or get too fixed in their ways, lest they become so complacent that they lose their ability to adapt to diversity or change.

When it is forgotten that conventional conceptions are conventional conceptions, and they are taken for objective facts that "everyone knows" and no one questions, then narrow-minded bigotry and blind prejudice can develop unopposed.

Lines 5–10:

> So being and nonbeing produce each other:
> difficulty and ease complement each other

These and the following lines represent the principle of relativity. This is understood to be the reason people should not have closed minds, as the opening lines of this chapter suggest: because the judgments of particular times, places, and people depend on subjective standpoints and therefore are not the same thing as objective truths in themselves.

3. Not Exalting Cleverness

Lines 1–2:

> Not exalting cleverness
> causes the people not to contend

Here cleverness is used in the sense of cunning and craft, such as that sought by contending lords hoping to learn ways of aggrandizing themselves and enlarging their holdings. Taoist philosophers did not believe that it was a good sign for society when cunning intellectuals were competing for the attention of the rich and powerful. According to Chen Jingyuan, this passage also means in general that people will not compete with you if you don't make much of your own cleverness. Su Che, who was a statesman as well as a poet and mystic, presents another view of this passage and the following passages that it introduces:

It's not that sage rulers don't employ the intelligent, only that they don't exalt them. They don't throw away goods that are hard to find, they just don't put high prices on them. They don't get rid of whatever is desirable, they just don't see it. Thus the intelligent are employed but the people don't compete; rare goods and desirable things are after all in plain view, but theft, robbery, and malicious disturbance do not arise.

Lines 7–8:

> Therefore the government of sages
> empties the mind and fills the middle

Emperor Huizong of the Song dynasty says, "Sage rulers have open minds, therefore they listen impartially, seeing all together without feelings of like and dislike. That their middles are full means they are content with enough and therefore have peace of mind, without greedy thoughts of craving."

Some Taoist yogis also understand this passage to refer to the rudimentary exercise of emptying the mind of thoughts and placing the attention in the abdomen or center of the body.

More generally, the passage is understood to refer to purification of the spirit and accumulation of energy.

4. *The Way Is Unimpeded Harmony*
Lines 6–7:

> harmonizes the light,
> assimilates to the world

An abbreviation of this passage is used in Chan Buddhism as a standard term for the practice of compassion, reentering the ordinary world after enlightenment. Taoists also understand it to refer to a postenlightenment exercise in being inconspicuous; the purpose of this was to refine consciousness through interaction with the world, and also to maintain a connection between the illuminate and the realm of human affairs. The last three lines represent the inner state of aloofness maintained while engaged in this exercise.

Line 8:

> it seems to be there

The presence of the Way can be intuitively sensed, but it cannot be pinned down anywhere.

Line 9:

> I don't know whose child it is

The ultimate source is inconceivable.

Line 10:

> before the creation of images

Intimation of the experience of the source comes through the awareness of the mind in its open state before the formulation of image and thought.

5. *Heaven and Earth*

Lines 1–4:

> Heaven and earth are not humane;
> they regard all beings as straw dogs.
> Sages are not humane;
> they see all people as straw dogs

Cheng Dachang says,

> This means everything has its time, then passes away, so there is continuous renewal. If you are a conscientious humanitarian, what are you going to do? Working for one impedes another; help one and you neglect a hundred. This kind of humanitarianism is both toilsome and trivial.
>
> Chuang-tzu said, "The supreme kindness has no familiarity; it should make you forget the world, and make the world forget you."

Cao Daozhong says, "Heaven, earth, and the sage are supremely humane, but they do not consider themselves humane, so it is said that they are not humane."

Lines 5–6:

> The space between heaven and earth is
> like bellows and pipes

Chen Jingyuan says, "The mind of the sage is empty and open, profoundly calm, dealing with the world harmoniously, like bellows taking in air, like pipes containing music."

Lines 9–11:

> The talkative reach their wits' end
> again and again;
> that is not as good as keeping centered

Emperor Huizong says, "By being careful of your inner state, shutting out externals, withdrawing your eyesight and reversing your hearing, you can go back to see the heart of heaven and earth. This is called keeping centered."

6. The Valley Spirit

Commentators define the valley spirit as open awareness, the mysterious female as a combination of firm sense and flexible receptivity. The valley spirit not dying means that the mirror awareness is not clouded by an accretion of attachment to mental objects and temporal conditioning. In the classic *Understanding Reality,* one of the great neo-Taoists wrote,

> If you want to attain the eternal immortality of the
> valley spirit,
> You must set the foundation on the mysterious female.
> Once true vitality returns to the room of yellow gold,
> The globe of spiritual light never parts.

Line 5:

> on the brink of existence

To say that the opening of the mysterious female is "on the brink of existence" is like the previous description of the Way as "seeming to be there," meaning that it cannot be nailed down as something you can point to as being just what it is.

Line 6:

> to put it into practice, don't try to force it

Deliberate intention and effort are in another domain of consciousness and do not touch the opening of the mysterious female, which cannot be forced because it eludes the contrivances of formal intellect, a different type of awareness. This passage is often cited in Taoist literature on meditation, referring to natural breathing and to mental poise.

8. *Higher Good Is like Water*

Chen Jingyuan says that water symbolizes having an open heart, dispassionately adapting to changes, according to the time. The latter part of this chapter, about goodness in words, government, work, and action, clearly shows that Taoism was not quietistic, introverted, or amoral, and not opposed to the original spirit of Confucianism.

9. *To Keep on Filling*

Lines 9–10:

> When one's work is accomplished honorably,
> to retire is the Way of heaven

Huang Mocai says, "No histories record where the ancient Wayfarers died. Isn't this a case of retiring when the path is done, to where no one can know?"

10. *Carrying Vitality and Consciousness*

I follow a reading of the Completely Real school of Taoism in translating the controversial opening of this chapter.

11. *Thirty Spokes*

This whole chapter is on the usefulness of the unused. The concept of "being" refers to what is explicit, or to forms being employed at a given time; "nonbeing" refers to what is implicit, or the formless universe of possibility unexpressed at a given time. "Being" is manifest operation; "nonbeing" is hidden potential. "Being" is the rational mode of mind; "nonbeing" is the intuitive mode. This chapter is not just philosophy, it is also an outline of a practical exercise used to switch from one mode of consciousness to another. The spokes and the pot stand for the realm of structure; space stands for the realm of open or spacelike awareness.

12. *Colors*

Lines 1–5:

> Colors blind people's eyes,
> sounds deafen their ears;
> flavors spoil people's palates,
> the chase and the hunt
> craze people's minds.

According to Chen Jingyuan, colors, sounds, and flavors all have legitimate functions in art, music, and diet, but they are perverted into superficial sensuous diversions. The chase and the hunt represent livelihood from the point of view of effort and struggle, which originally have a function in human life but become diverted into ambition. With ambition cannibalizing effort and struggle, livelihood becomes a rat race. People degenerate under these conditions: no longer do they use the energies of sense and feeling to propel themselves into greater understanding and attunement with subtler phenomena such as principles, balances, and harmonies; on the contrary, degenerating humans diffuse energies through the habit of dwelling on the senses and feelings themselves.

Lines 6–7:

> goods hard to obtain
> make people's actions harmful

The usual interpretation is that people become covetous, competitive, and thieving when they learn to desire precious objects. A special interpretation is that it is better to seek the inner alchemy than to become too eager for external remedies. This means that the various arts of Taoism can be made into objects of seeking on a lesser plane; the more avidly and competitively sought the more esoteric they are made to seem.

Lines 8–10:

> Therefore sages work for the middle
> and not the eyes,
> leaving the latter and taking the former

Emperor Huizong says,

> *Earth* is the middle of the eight trigrams, because it is richly supportive and accepting. *Fire* is the eyes, meaning consciously looking outwardly. Rich support and acceptance takes in all, but consciously looking outwardly doesn't reach everything. Sages use the world as a measure, so they take this accommodating middle; they do not order every single affair or examine every single thing, so they leave those outward-looking eyes. Chuangtzu said, "No robber is so great as consciousness of virtue, and eyes in that consciousness."

Liu Qi says,

> The middle means inner spaciousness, the eyes mean viewing externals. Sages withdraw their vision and reverse their hearing, going back to the source and returning to life, governing the inner and not the outer, seeking it in themselves and not in others.
>
> Here the eyes do not mean objective vision, only subjective vision. Hearing does not mean objective hearing, only subjective hearing.

13. *Favor and Disgrace*
Line 1:

> Favor and disgrace seem alarming

Chen Jingyuan says,

> This is for people of middling capacities only. People of middling knowledge consider possible danger when in a secure situation, and when favored they are mindful of the possibility of

disgrace. Therefore they are as if alarmed, because of the depth of their prudence. The movement of the heart is not the same as alarm, so the text says "seem alarming."

Ye Mengde reads the line,

> When favor is disgraced, you may awaken

He comments,

> People of the world are not alarmed by favor, but they are alarmed by disgrace. When favor becomes excessive, it is inevitably disgraceful; while the disgraced eventually are restored to favor. If you see favor as like disgrace, and wake up, then you know that where there is favor there is always disgrace.

Line 2:

> high status greatly afflicts your person

Su Che says, "High status afflicts your person when used for personal indulgence."

Other commentators also read the word for "person" in its meaning of "body," observing the stress placed on the body under the pressures of life in high society. The word used in this chapter for person, self, and body here includes the material and social being and condition.

Lines 13–18:

> Therefore those who embody nobility
> to act for the sake of the world
> seem to be able to draw the world to them,
> while those who embody love
> to act for the sake of the world
> seem to be worthy of the trust of the world

Chen Xianggu says, "If you work for the world egotistically, presuming to be noble, that is not a rallying point for the world. If you work for the world egotistically presuming to be loving, that is not the key to the trust of the world. That is why the text says 'seem.'"

Ye Mengde reads,

> Those who work for the world with self-importance

only seem to be worthy of the world's investment;
those who work for the world with self-love
only seem to be worthy of the world's trust.

He comments,

Even if you do not value high status, if you are self-important
you may win the world but will not dare to look upon it as a
journey. This is not the type of person in whom the world can
be invested. Even if you do not love favor, if you love yourself you
may win the world but you will not dare to take care of it like a
cottage. This is not the type of person to whom the world can be
entrusted.

14. When You Look at It You Don't See It

This is an ode symbolizing a mystical exercise. The first eight
lines describe the essential bridge linking the two sides of the
mind; the ninth and most abstruse line epitomizes the two
sides:

above is not bright, below is not dark

Emperor Huizong says of this line, "The metaphysical is
unfathomable, mysterious, and hard to know. This is called
most sacred, and this is the reason it is 'not bright.' The physical is orderly and regular; this is called the effective way, so it
is 'not dark.'"

The ode concludes with emphasis on holding "the Ancient
Way," defined by Chen Jingyuan as the formless, nameless
source of the universe. The chapter concludes by saying that it
is only when you know the ancient, that is, the eternal, that
this can be called a basic cycle of the Way: a basic cycle of the
Way has two aspects, knowledge of temporal reality and
knowledge of eternal reality.

15. Skilled Warriors of Old

Lines 18–19:

Just because of not wanting fullness,
it is possible to use to the full and not make anew

By accepting what is and making the best use of every situation, life can be fulfilled without a constant demand for more.

16. *Attain the Climax of Emptiness*
This chapter consists of meditation directions.

Line 4:

> I thereby observe the return

"Thereby" refers to emptiness and quiet. "The return" is interpreted by some to mean the return of pure primal positive energy after quieting and emptying the mind. Others interpret it to mean the return of all things to their origins, calmly observed with an open mind by the Taoist.

Line 18:

> not endangered by physical death

This passage is another indication of the ancient roots of the idea of spiritual or metaphysical immortality, later elaborated by Taoist alchemists.

17. *Very Great Leaders*
According to the earliest historical account of Lao-tzu as the author of the *Tao Te Ching,* he is supposed to have told Confucius, "A good merchant hides his goods and appears to have nothing; a skilled craftsman leaves no traces."

18. *When the Great Way Is Deserted*
Cheng Dachang says, citing *Chuang-tzu,*

> In the age of perfect virtue, the leaders were like pointing branches, the people were like wild deer. They were upright, but they didn't know to consider that justice. They loved each other, but they didn't know to consider that humanity. Therefore their actions left no traces, their affairs left no history.

19. *Eliminate Sagacity, Abandon Knowledge*
Lines 1–2:

> Eliminate sagacity, abandon knowledge,
> and the people benefit a hundredfold

Intellectuals were constantly trying to sell their ideas to powerful people. These intellectuals apparently often had little more than mythology for data on which to base their hypotheses and theories, but that does not seem to have mattered much to some of them. If such intellectuals could persuade the influential to try their schemes, the populace could be in for some hard times as guinea pigs for their political and economic experiments.

Lines 3–4:

> Eliminate humanitarianism, abandon duty,
> and the people return to familial love

As for humanitarianism and duty, like sagacity and knowledge taking on the special meanings of cunning and craft, these terms also came to have peculiar undertones. Humanitarianism and duty turned into expressions used by the elite to forgive each other for being despotic tyrants and support each other in their pretensions.

Lines 5–6:

> Eliminate craft, abandon profit,
> and theft will no longer exist

Crafts and commerce were also thrown out of balance by gross inequalities in socioeconomic power. With artisans and merchants attracted to competition for the patronage of the well-to-do and their luxury trade, the technology and economy of the general populace tended to stagnate and were even further burdened by increasing taxes levied on the people to support the upper classes accustomed to luxury.

Lines 7–9:

> These three become insufficient
> when used for embellishment
> causing there to be attachments

The three are (1) sagacity and knowledge; (2) humanitarianism and duty; (3) craft and profit. When these are used superficially, for personal aggrandizement and competition, not for the welfare of society, then they lose their worth. All are useful at some time, but are turned into objects of striving and contention in themselves, not used as civilizing influences.

20. *Detach from Learning and You Have No Worries*

Here "learning" means habituation to convention. Chen Jingyuan says, "Modern learning is superficial. Detachment from learning does not mean not learning anything at all, it means maintaining the natural essence of mind." Lin Dong says, "If you give up the original natural essence of mind and seek the Way outside, there is something special called learning, which is all externally oriented. Only by detachment from this learning can you be worry free: this is attained spontaneously by following essential nature; it is not learned."

Line 2:

> How far apart are yes and yeah?

The Legalist versions of the text have different (but physically similar) characters for the one I translate "yeah." Those other characters mean to holler, blame, get angry at. Some scholars prefer this reading, interpreting it as meaning strong disagreement in contrast to agreement, to parallel the opposition of good and bad in the next line. I am inclined to think this misses the Taoistic point of these lines. Everyone is aware that *yes* and *yeah* have the same meaning but differ by convention: this is used to open the question to what extent *good* and *bad* as conventional definitions actually apply to the reality at hand. Things, ideas, acts, or people that appear different may be basically equal but more or less socially acceptable in a given historical context. When the two questions asked in the text here are construed as exactly parallel in structure, there is a tendency to jump to the conclusion that Taoism is saying good and bad are one, or that there is no good or bad. See again the second line of chapter 2, which could be written, "When 'everyone knows' good is good, this is not good."

Line 4:

The things people fear cannot but be feared

This line is also changed in the one extant Legalist version of it, to "[If you] are feared by others, you cannot but therefore fear others."

The standard version has puzzled some Western translators, who prefer to add a suppositional interrogative, "Why should one fear what others fear?" This is probably based on the idea that Taoism preaches transcendence of convention. Linguistically speaking, the interrogative is not one of the classes of particles commonly omitted as understood in Classical and Literary Chinese. As an idea, "the things people fear cannot but be feared" deals with the nature and function of fear itself, and is both inwardly and outwardly connected with the antiwar passages in this same text. People in fear do fearsome things, which further escalate fear, which increases insane activity, and so on. War is an example and an illustration of this process. My sense is that the Legalist version is a legitimate adaptation of Taoism to the Legalist way as well as to the Strategic and Martial schools of thought with which it was connected, but I doubt the "Why should one fear what others fear?" reading, on the grounds that it is linguistically unsound and philosophically questionable in both theory and practice. The aloofness, detachment, and buoyancy described in the following lines refer to an extra inner capacity that in one sense may be said to be cultivated precisely out of fear of what people fear. Those who cultivate such an inner capacity solely out of that fear, however, may that much more easily wind up in an antinomian attitude.

Line 27:

> I value seeking food from the mother

There are different layers of meaning in this key line. It means taking psychological and physical nourishment from the source of energy, not from the excitement of reactions set off by its productions. On a parallel but more subtle level, it also means taking input directly from primal awareness of the world, as in "being is the mother of all things."

Su Che says, "The Way is the mother of all things. Most people forget about the Way as they follow after things, but sages stand aloof from things and take to the Way as the fundamental source, just like a suckling child feeding from its mother."

Daozhen says,

> Most people seek things outside themselves, I alone feed on energy within. Energy is the mother, spirit is the child. When spirit does not leave energy, and energy does not leave the physical body, child and mother accompany each other continuously. Eventually the higher and the lower naturally settle. It is wrong to block this. This is a simple summary of hygiene, the art of keeping life together.

21. *The Countenance of Great Virtue*

In Taoist meditation, the states represented by words like *nothingness* and *silence* are not themselves the Way, but are ways to the Way. Material from the third through eighth lines is standard in Taoist contemplative lore; herein the difference between nothingness and the Way is clear.

Lines 11, 12:

> all beauties

The expression "all beauties" can also be read "all beginnings."

Su Che says, "All beauties pass away, but the eternal Way remains. The evanescence of beauties is seen in the perspective of the Way."

22. Be Tactful and You Remain Whole
Lines 19–22:

> Is it empty talk, the old saying
> that tact keeps you whole?
> When truthfulness is complete,
> it still resorts to this

"This" means tactfulness; complete truthfulness still resorts to tact. Applied to both teaching situations and social situations, this is the same principle as the Buddhist *upaya-kaushalya*, "skill in means," exercised deliberately by the enlightened to make contact with people of different mentalities.

23. To Speak Rarely Is Natural
Line 12:

> those who assimilate to loss are also happy to gain it

The inner meaning of loss here is reduction of selfishness, pride, egoism, greed, and possessiveness; assimilation to loss can refer to a purely internal process or to the process of using external loss, when it happens, as a means of approaching loss in the inner liberative sense. See also chapters 42 and 48.

24. Those on Tiptoe Don't Stand Up
The general point of the first two lines is that maximum exertion cannot be sustained.

Line 8:

> (Some) people (may) disdain them

Ye Mengde says that the text says "Some people" (or "People may") because not everyone has the sense to disdain overconsumption and excess activity.

25. *Something Undifferentiated*
Line 15:

> kingship is also great

Kingship stands for the human order. The Way is thought of as the progenitrix of heaven and earth, which stand for the spiritual and natural orders; the human order stands between, and shares in the qualities of, the spiritual and natural orders of heaven and earth.

26. *Gravity Is the Root of Lightness*
An inner meaning of this idea that applies to the practice of spiritual sublimation is that effective management of ordinary necessities frees the mind for higher things. The second and third couplets describe the effective combination of detachment and involvement. The last two couplets depict the wrong kind of combination.

27. *Good Works*
Lines 10–11:

> [sages] always consider it good to save beings,
> so that there are no wasted beings

The word for "(living) beings" also means "things." Sociology and ecology were closely related in classical Taoism.

28. *Know the Male*
The word for "know" also means to manage. The male and female, the white and black, the glorious and ignominious, stand for intellect and intuition, form and emptiness, doing and nondoing, the mundane and the transcendental. The complete human being, in Taoist terms, is master of both these sides of the human potential but always reverts to the dark, quiet, unknown side for restoration of energy and spirit; "Return is the movement of the Way."

Lines 4, 9, 15:

eternal power

The word for power used here is the same as virtue or charisma and means spiritual power rather than material power.

29. *Should You Want*

A variant text starts this chapter with the lines, "Generals want to take the world, and fight with weapons for it; I see they will not manage to finish." The standard text, with which the Legalist version agrees, can also be read in a similar manner to say, "Generals want to take the world, and strive for this." The first character can be read semantically as "generals," or functionally as a suppositional particle. Either way it makes sense, but to construe the first character as a particle results in a wider meaning than just military attempts to take the world.

30. *Assisting Human Leaders with the Way*
Line 13:

If you peak in strength, you then age

This theme is reiterated in several different ways throughout the text; the outflow of energy cannot be kept at a maximum all the time without depleting the system.

31. *Fine Weapons*
Lines 2–3:

people may despise [weapons],
so those with the Way do not dwell with them

As in chapter 24, the literal "people may" is translated something like "all people" by those who expect sentimental dogmatics. The evident fact is, however, that not all people do despise weaponry; those with the Way go along with the most sensible.

Lines 15–16:

> The left is favored for auspicious things,
> the right for things of ill omen

It is interesting to note that this pattern of association is opposite to the globally more common tendency to regard the right as auspicious and the left as sinister. So much for universal archetypes. Even in later Taoist tradition, the expression "left-hand path" is derogatory.

32. *The Way Is Eternally Nameless*
Lines 2–3:

> Though simplicity is small,
> the world cannot subordinate it

"The world cannot" may also be read as "no one can," and there is a variant textual reading that says "no one dares." Daozhen says, "Simplicity is not a function or a position, not a name or number; it has no fixed division of upper and lower. It is before categorization of people, so no one can rule over it."

Lines 8–9:

> No humans command it;
> it is even by nature

This reading refers to natural order. The statement can also be used as a symbol of ideal human order, in which sense it can be read, "The people even themselves, without anyone commanding them." This represents the idea of the unspoken influence of the charisma of sages.

33. *Those Who Know Others*
Line 8:

> those who die without perishing live long

The Legalist texts read, "Those who die but are not forgotten are long lived." The Taoist version is generally understood to refer to mystical consciousness, the Legalist to social consciousness. Taoist contemplatives speak of the death of mind and the life of spirit, by which they mean the subordination of the limited human mentality to the more encompassing consciousness of the Way.

34. The Great Way Is Universal

Line 2:

it can apply to the left or the right

This means that the Way can be used to attain both spiritual and mundane aims.

35. Holding the Great Image

The Great Image is a symbol of the Tao, or Way; it is called flavorless, invisible, and inaudible, in reference to the consciousness of the Way, an awareness more subtle than material sense yet present and effective.

36. Should You Want to Contain

This chapter is highly prized by strategists. Wang Yiqing says, "When you see forced expansion, you know there will be shrinkage, and when you see a display of strength, you know there is weakness."

Line 13:

the effective tools of the nation

This expression is understood by commentators to refer to generals, to a nation's means of governing its people, and/or to strategy and state secrets. On the individual level, to say that the effective tools of the nation shouldn't be shown to people means that one should not display one's talents at the drop of a hat.

37. The Way Is Always Uncontrived

The second century B.C. Taoist group known as the Masters of Huainan explicitly rejected the vulgar reading of "inaction" for *wu-wei,* or noncontrivance.

38. *Higher Virtue Is Not Ingratiating*

Or, "higher virtue is not virtuous," in two senses: first, that it excludes expectation of reward, personal presumption, or proprietary sentiments in regard to virtue; second, that it does not consist of specific "virtues" as defined in dogmatic moral systems. The word for virtue also means gratitude and reward. According to this chapter, only the Way and higher virtue are uncreated or uncontrived; lower virtue, higher humanity, higher duty, and higher courtesy are all "done," and all but higher humanity involve specific method. Higher humanity is created, or done, but cannot be fabricated. Higher humanity (or humaneness), higher duty (or justice), and higher courtesy are treated in detail in the Taoist classic *Wen-tzu,* which claims to derive from the same source as the *Tao Te Ching,* the teaching of Lao-tzu or the Old Master(s).

39. *Ancient Attainment of Unity*

Line 21:

> there is no praise in repeated praise

A variant reading says, "Ultimate praise has no praise."

Line 22:

> they don't want to be like jewels or like stones

Lords (here symbolic of sages) do not want to be evaluated by fixed conventions, or assigned to fixed categories.

43. *What Is Softest in the World*

This chapter might be said to express what Taoist strategists and political scientists generally consider the supreme tactical skill.

45. *Great Completeness Seems Incomplete*

Lines 8–9:

> Movement overcomes cold,
> stillness overcomes heat

This refers to the process of adjusting physical and/or mental equilibrium.

47. *Without Even Going out the Door*

This chapter refers to abstract and intuitive knowledge, in contrast to formal intellectual knowledge, which is "less the further out it goes."

48. *For Learning You Gain Daily*
Line 2:

> Losing and losing

Losing here means shedding psychological barriers to the reality of the Way, barriers created by self-assertion and the accretions of mundane conditioning.

49. *Sages Have No Fixed Mind*
Line 11:

> they cloud their minds for the world

Read in this manner, this line means that sages are not petty or picayune in judging people; similarly, greathearted saints in Buddhism are sometimes said to be blind, insofar as they do not condemn or reject people for their shortcomings and weaknesses.

Another way of reading the line is "they unify minds for the world," in the sense of uniting the world in spirit.

Line 12:

> all people pour into their ears and eyes

Read in this way, the line means that sages regard all people. It can also be read, "the people all focus their ears and eyes [on sages]," in the sense of looking up to sages for examples.

50. *From Life into Death*
Lines 2, 3, 6:

> three out of ten

This is interpreted by some commentators to mean ten and three, or thirteen; others read three of ten, or thirty percent. Those who read thirteen give various lists of so many parts of the physical body, or so many psychological experiences. Su Che says,

> The followers of life are those who use things to extract the vitalities in order to nourish themselves. Followers of death are those who deplete themselves with sense impacts. Furthermore, to know how to act but not how to desist, to know how to speak but not how to be silent, to know how to think but not how to forget, thereby heading for exhaustion, are the "dying grounds on which they are agitated."

Those who read three out of ten, or thirty percent, interpret it to mean that only three out of ten people are in accord with any principle. One commentary places the chapter in the context of the era and interprets it in terms of militarism and warfare.

Line 17:

> they have no dying ground

To have no dying ground means not clinging to anything and therefore not being pinned down anywhere, thus having no points of vulnerability.

52. *The World Has a Beginning*
Lines 2–6:

> mother . . . child

The mother is the mother energy, the source of being, the fecund aspect of the Tao. The child is the realm of ideas and inventions, the world of myriad forms. Knowing the nature of the child as derivative and renewable, you keep the mother, the primary source of renewal; thus as the source energy survives the passing of its creations, humankind can keep the mother alive generation after generation.

On another level, "once you know the child" means when you have lived life fully; "you return to keep the mother" means ultimately concentrating on the source of being. "Not perishing though the body die" is the result of this specialized concentration, with the disappearance of consciousness of physical individuality through absorption in the mother, the source of being. Something similar is practiced in Pure Land Buddhism.

Line 8:

> Close your eyes, shut your doors

This refers to inner absorption in the primal.

Line 10:

> Open your eyes, carry out your affairs

This refers to outer involvement in the temporal.

Lines 14–15:

> Using the shining radiance,
> you return again to the light,
> not leaving anything to harm yourself

The shining radiance is the discursive intellect; the light is immediate awareness. Always being able to return to the beginning, without becoming fixated on the objects or products of discursive intellect, forestalls potentially harmful biases and obsessions.

Line 16:

> This is called entering the eternal

The word for "entering" also means reaching, relying on, and being based upon. Another version says "learning/practicing the eternal." The unrefracted light of the immediate awareness of the basic ground of consciousness is called the eternal because its essence is not modified by temporal conditioning.

53. *Causing One Flashes*

Lines 1–3:

> Causing one flashes of knowledge
> to travel the Great Way,
> only its application demands care

The application of the Way causes flashes of knowledge that light up the signposts along the Way. Therefore the quality of practice and the quality of realization and understanding are interdependent.

Lines 4–5:

> The Great Way is quite even,
> yet people prefer byways

The Great Way involves cultivation of comprehensive understanding of human nature and potential, but there is also popular demand for mechanical systems of salvation or consciousness-altering techniques.

56. *Those Who Know Do Not Say*

Lines 1–2:

> Those who know do not say;
> those who say do not know

This statement refers specifically to inconceivable experiences and extraordinary perceptions such as may result from mystical exercises. More generally, it suggests that experts have no need to flaunt their knowledge and that it is the dilettantes who are always showing off.

Lines 3–6:

> Close . . . shut . . . blunt . . . resolve

These lines refer to the practice of switching off or standing apart from conceptual consciousness. This is done to enter the realm of direct perception. The next two lines, "harmonize the light, assimilate to the world," refer to integration of the enhanced and purified awareness thus attained with the everyday practicalities of the ordinary world.

58. *When the Government Is Unobtrusive*
Lines 5–6:

> Calamity is what fortune depends upon;
> fortune is what calamity subdues.

We seldom realize the blessings we have enjoyed until we have troubles. Those who know they are lucky without having bad luck are those who are really lucky.

60. *Governing a Large Nation Is like Cooking Small Fry*
They say the best way to cook small fry is not to stir too much.

Line 8:

> sages do not harm the people either

In this passage the word *sage* is evidently used particularly in its special meaning of "ruler."

Lines 9–10:

> Because the two do not harm each other,
> their virtues ultimately combine

The two are the spiritual and human worlds; humans were believed to get cooperation from unseen powers when in harmony with Nature.

62. *The Way Is the Pivot of All Things*
Lines 4–6:

> Fine words can be sold,
> honored acts can oppress people;
> why should people who are not good abandon them?

Hypocrites may put on pretenses of virtue to get their own way, and this passage points up the danger of becoming for all practical purposes completely hardened in such an attitude. Another line of interpretation reads, "Fine words can be made public, noble acts can be applied to others; why should people who are not good [or, what is bad about people] be abandoned?" This way of reading speaks of the universal benefit of the Way, even for those who are not good, and indeed of the need to embrace the unregenerate with fine words and noble deeds.

63. Do Nondoing
Lines 9–10:

> The most difficult things in the world
> must be done while they are easy

This is echoed in the classic on strategy, *The Art of War,* drawing on Taoist tradition: "Those who win every battle are not really skillful — those who render others' armies helpless without fighting are the best of all" ("Planning a Siege").

Also, "In ancient times those known as good warriors prevailed when it was easy to prevail" ("Formation").

64. What Is at Rest Is Easy to Hold
Lines 27–28:

> They learn not learning
> to recover from people's excesses

Sages learn how to be unaffected by their surroundings, "to recover from people's excesses," always returning to innocence.

67. Everyone Says
A variant reading of the introductory passages has, "My Way seems very unworthy. It seems unworthy because of its greatness. If its worth were of long standing, it would be trivialized." It seems that whatever has been stored securely in a convenient category, whatever it may be, thereby inevitably comes to be taken for granted. This common characteristic of the human

mind appears to have originated in a sort of superelaboration or hyperextension of the natural screening function of the brain.

Lines 16–17:

> By reason of frugality,
> one can be broad

Breadth refers to capacity, versatility, generosity, and function. The Masters of Huainan say, "Those who gain the benefit of power have very little in the way of holdings and very much in the way of responsibility. What they maintain is very restricted, what they control is very broad" (*The Tao of Politics*).

78. *The Most Flexible Thing in the World*
Lines 11–12:

> those who can take on the disgrace of nations
> are leaders of lands

The Masters of Huainan recount an interesting and amusing story to illustrate this paradoxical saying. It seems that at one time the leaders of a certain state learned that their neighbors were planning to invade and seize territory. Upon receiving this report, the head of state and his ministers began to apologize to each other and try to take the blame upon themselves, each claiming to be responsible for this state of affairs, the ruler insisting that his rulership must have been faulty, the ministers pronouncing their own administration deficient. When a spy at court who witnessed these proceedings reported the incident to the ruler of the neighboring state, it was decided that it would not be prudent to invade a state whose rulership and administration had such an acute sense of individual responsibility.

79. *Harmonize Bitter Enemies*
Lines 1–3:

> When you harmonize bitter enemies,
> yet resentment is sure to linger,
> how can this be called good?

It is difficult to avoid thinking, in this connection, of the martial history of the world in the twentieth century, particularly of regional conflicts facilitated by certain characteristics of the peace treaties ending the two world wars; of more than forty years of cold war; and of the economic and political relics of the colonial era.

80. *A Small State Has Few People*
Lines 17–18:

> they make it so that the people
> have never gone back and forth

Life in ideal states runs so well that people do not even think of going anywhere else.

81. *True Words Are Not Beautiful*
The point may be made more forcefully by rendering the opening lines, "True words are not beautified; beautified words are not true." There is a Chinese proverb that says, "Truthful words offend the ears." "True words are not beautiful" in the sense that they are not there that way to flatter the ego; "beautiful words are not true" if they are there that way just for appearances.

Notes to Chuang-tzu

1. Freedom

The Giant Fish and Bird

The giant fish symbolizes the hidden potential for higher development; the giant bird symbolizes this potential in action. The transformation symbolizes the process of activation; the water, air, and flight symbolize the cultivation of the degrees of vitality, energy, and consciousness necessary to carry out the process of transformation.

The locust, pigeon, and marsh quail represent pedestrian minds clinging to their limited subjectivity.

The philosopher Jung of Sung represents partial transcendence: the ability to be mentally independent of convention without the ability to act constructively.

Master Lieh represents the stage of transcendence of worldly things and initiation into the inconceivable possibilities of mind, but not yet reaching the ultimate Taoist experience of intimate union with the workings of the universe.

King Yao and Hsü Yu

King Yao was a legendary ruler, symbolic of wise government. Hsü Yu was an individual illuminate living in obscurity. The story represents the preeminence of spiritual mastery over mastery of the world, of self-mastery over mastery of others.

Chien Wu and Lien Shu

The spiritual people spoken of in this story represent stabilization of the spirit, resulting in overall improvement of health throughout the physical and social bodies.

Hui-tzu and Chuang-tzu

The huge gourd stands for the human being; its usefulness or otherwise depends on its use. To "make a coracle of it" means to "hollow" it out, in the sense of becoming inwardly empty and open; to "sail on the rivers and lakes" means to be free in the midst of the world.

The enormous tree represents a mind beyond convention. To be "useless" means to be unexploitable.

2.   On Equalizing Things

Tzu-ch'i and Tzu-yu

To be "oblivious of body and soul" means to entertain no image of person; to "forget oneself" means to entertain no image of ego.

The pipes of heaven, earth, and humanity represent differences in the states of beings; the wind playing the pipes represents the underlying unity of the vital energy of life. Taoists try to become aware of this and harmonize with it.

The Taoist master Fu-kuei-tzu says, "Humans are the most intelligent of beings, yet they change their attitudes in various unequal ways, because the real director is not present. If people would get the sense of the real director, then they would not be guided by the subjective psyche, but would spontaneously be on the Way."

Diffused Brilliance

Fu-kuei-tzu says, "When you think about the beginning, before there were even things, before there were even boundaries, you find there is no affirmation or negation, no right or wrong; so how could there be completeness or lack? Thus the harpist, the tuner, and the philosopher [who were attached to their particular arts], all wound up spending their lives on sophistry.

"And yet even so there is still no completeness or lack. That is why what sages aim for is diffused brilliance. In the context of the human way, diffused brilliance is called 'absence of images,' and in the context of the way of Nature it is called 'living light.'"

The Hair Tip and the Mountain
This selection describes relativity, and the relativity of relativity. When you objectify absolute unity as a topic of deliberate attention, it becomes relative to the subjective standpoint from which it is discussed; and when you think about this relationship, that too becomes relative to the way you think of it.

"Not getting anywhere" means revolving within the limitations of subjective assessments. "Going from nonbeing to being" refers to transition from stillness to movement or nothing to something; the "third point" is the pivot, or transition from movement, or something, back to stillness, or nothing. To go "from being to being" means to go from movement to movement, or something to something, without returning to the zero point, thus building up a complex chain of ongoing influences and effects.

3.   Mastery of Nurturing Life
The Death of Lao Tan
Lao Tan is ordinarily identified with Lao-tzu, transmitter of the *Tao Te Ching*. He appears several times in the inner chapters of *Chuang-tzu*. Fu-kuei-tzu says, "People born in the world who do not know how to leap out of the cage of passive and active forces are all marionettes, and the strings of the marionettes are all in the hands of God. When God picks them up, they are born; if God does not hold them up, they die. People who are immune to the influence of sorrow and joy cannot be constrained by Creation, so God lets go of their strings, and their life is equal to Nature."

Kindling a Fire
Fu-kuei-tzu says, "The physical body is like fuel; fire is the spirit. Those who nurture the physical body are nurturing life; this is keeping the fuel. Those who nurture the spirit are nurturing the master of nurturing life; this is keeping the fire."

4. The Human World

Fu-kuei-tzu says of this chapter, "The whole book of Chuang-tzu is centered on transcending the world, but people who have transcended the world since ancient times have always seen through the affairs of the world first, for only thus could they cut through to rise above the world. Therefore this chapter goes back to use the task of involvement with the world as a vehicle for teachings on transcending the world."

The Mantis, Tiger Keepers, and Horse Lover

Fu-kuei-tzu says, "The mantis represents how people with fine talents should be careful of what they say. The tiger keepers symbolize how the feelings of the populace should be mentioned tactfully. The horse lover is a symbol of how a little impatience can ruin great plans."

The Giant Trees, the Hunchback, and the Madman

Fu-kuei-tzu says that the giant trees "kept their lives because they were not usable as timber," and the hunchback "sustained himself because he was handicapped." He adds, "As for those who are detached from their own virtues, they bury their names, conceal their illumination, and do not show them off. And how about when the vital spirit is completely stable?"

5. Tallying with Fulfillment of Virtue

Fu-kuei-tzu says, "This chapter defines virtue as internal and physical form as external; physical form may be forgotten, but virtue is not to be forgotten. Virtue is based on keeping the source and preserving the beginning. The seat of consciousness is where the spirit is stored and the vitality is collected, the spiritual house of the human being, the place where the source is kept and the beginning preserved. Anyone who would nurture virtue must begin from here. Once virtue is full within, it naturally shows corresponding effects outwardly; heaven and earth become your office, myriad things become your treasury."

Wang T'ai
Chopping a foot off was a form of punishment in ancient China. Tyrants apparently used to have the feet chopped off of independent thinkers who said things that might influence people in ways not amenable to the interests of tyrants. Other people, real criminals, also got their feet chopped off, so the inner reality of the individual was not necessarily evidenced by his or her outward appearance. This is the point of the story: seeing beyond the ephemeral and the superficial to the real and the profound.

Shen-t'u Chia
Another sage who had run afoul of a despot is here taken to task by someone who regards superficial appearances. The superficialist suggests that there must be something wrong with the maimed man, and he also takes him to task for associating familiarly with his social superiors.

Egalitarian ideals are very prominent in ancient Taoist social and political thought. Their mode of "class" distinction is based on inner qualities of character and wisdom rather than circumstances of birth.

Confucius and Lao Tan
Fu-kuei-tzu says, "We have heard that character and virtue are internal, whereas the body is external; and the external and the internal have long been out of contact. Is it like the wise to forget the internal and seek the external? Chuang-tzu brings out another man with a foot chopped off in a parable to illustrate how preserving the body intact is not as good as preserving character intact."

Here Confucius and Lao Tan (Lao-tzu) represent two sides of consciousness, with different views of the world: the maimed man here symbolizes frustration in the attempt of one side to communicate with the other, like the artistic side of an individual being suppressed by the logical side.

6. The Great Teacher of the Source

Fu-kuei-tzu says, "The 'great teacher of the source' is the basic original spirit in human beings. Everyone has it, but no one knows how to take it as a source and a teacher; that is why Chuang-tzu points it out in many ways."

Hsi Wei, Fu Hsi, K'an Pei, P'ing I, Chien Wu, and the others were ancient chieftains, culture heroes, nature spirits, and so on, who attained their qualities and stature by the Tao; they represent transformation and ennoblement of humanity by communion with the cosmic reality of the Way.

Fu-kuei-tzu says, "The only resort is the existence of the Way that is its own basis and its own root. Ghosts and deities need it to be spiritualized, heaven and earth need it to be born. Nothing is as high or as deep, nothing lasts as long or is as old. Chieftains need it to be chieftains; the sun, moon, planets, stars, mountains, and rivers need it to be the sun, moon, planets, stars, mountains, and rivers; immortals, adepts, sages, and saints need it to be immortals, adepts, sages, and saints."

Tzu-ch'i and Nü-yü

The spiritual lineage of Nü-yü, "Son of Assistant Writing, Grandson of Thoroughly Versed," and so on, ultimately deriving from "High Void" and "Uncertain Beginning," symbolizes a course of Taoist learning, from study and understanding of the principles and processes to pragmatic experience of the subtleties.

Mysterious Darkness, High Void, and Uncertain Beginning have meanings in both metaphysics and physics. Mysterious Darkness is defined as the beginning of the energy massing leading up to what we call the Big Bang; in the High Void there is no energy mass, only abstract nature; the Uncertain Beginning is the unknowable, which nevertheless continues to pervade the post–Big Bang universe at the subatomic level.

I-erh-tzu and Hsü Yu

Hsü Yu appeared before as the ancient sage who refused to accept the throne of China when it was offered to him. When here he speaks of "my teacher" as "it," he is referring to the Tao, or Way, itself.

Yen Hui and Confucius
Yen Hui is famous in both Taoist and Confucian literature as the most morally and spiritually advanced of the disciples of Confucius. "Sitting forgetting," is a term for a class of meditation techniques aimed at transcending the limitations of conditioned consciousness.

Confucius represents reason; when he says he would follow Yen Hui because of the latter's assimilation to the universal, this means that reason, in the Taoist view, needs to be completed by direct gnostic experience of reality without the interposition of subjectivity.

7. Responsive Leadership
Fu-kuei-tzu says, "The overall message of this chapter is based on Lao-tzu's saying, 'Leaders find their model in Nature; Nature finds its model in the Way; the Way finds its model in spontaneity.' If we want leaders today to be responsive, they must also do likewise."

Teeth Missing and Royal Child
Fu-kuei-tzu says that when Royal Child was questioned about the Way of governing the world and answered that he didn't know, this had the sense of what an ancient classic calls "unconsciously, unknowingly, obeying the laws of God."

Fu-kuei-tzu also says that the ancient emperor T'ai "would consider himself a horse or an ox" because he was "merged with the whole of Nature," and he "never entered into repudiating people" because "when you attain the Way you forget the Way."

Bearing Self and Crazy Chariot-Grabber
Other stories represent the usefulness and also the limitations of certain ideas and attitudes espoused by Confucius. This story, and the next two, are Taoist critiques of simplistic Confucian political rhetoric.

167

The last few stories talk about the processes of evolution and involution, and how humankind has the potential to free itself and also to stifle itself.